199

Internet-Based Businesses You Can Start with Less than One Thousand Dollars:

Secrets, Techniques, and Strategies Ordinary People Use Every Day to Make Millions

by Sharon L. Cohen

with a foreword by
Bill Askenburg

Artisan & Proprietor,
New England Birdhouse,
www.NewEnglandBirdhouse.com

We recently lost our beloved pet "Bear," who was not only our best and dearest friend but also the "Vice President of Sunshine" here at Atlantic Publishing. He did not receive a salary but worked tirelessly 24 hours a day to please his parents. Bear was a rescue dog that turned around and showered myself, my wife, Sherri, his grandparents
Jean, Bob, and Nancy, and every person and animal he met (maybe not rabbits) with friendship and love. He made a lot of people smile every day.

We wanted you to know that a portion of the profits of this book will be donated to The Humane Society of the United States. *–Douglas & Sherri Brown*

The human-animal bond is as old as human history. We cherish our animal companions for their unconditional affection and acceptance. We feel a thrill when we glimpse wild creatures in their natural habitat or in our own backyard.

Unfortunately, the human-animal bond has at times been weakened. Humans have exploited some animal species to the point of extinction.

The Humane Society of the United States makes a difference in the lives of animals here at home and worldwide. The HSUS is dedicated to creating a world where our relationship with animals is guided by compassion. We seek a truly humane society in which animals are respected for their intrinsic value, and where the human-animal bond is strong.

Want to help animals? We have plenty of suggestions. Adopt a pet from a local shelter, join The Humane Society and be a part of our work to help companion animals and wildlife. You will be funding our educational, legislative, investigative and outreach projects in the U.S. and across the globe.

Or perhaps you'd like to make a memorial donation in honor of a pet, friend or relative? You can through our Kindred Spirits program. And if you'd like to contribute in a more structured way, our Planned Giving Office has suggestions about estate planning, annuities, and even gifts of stock that avoid capital gains taxes.

Maybe you have land that you would like to preserve as a lasting habitat for wildlife. Our Wildlife Land Trust can help you. Perhaps the land you want to share is a backyard— that's enough. Our Urban Wildlife Sanctuary Program will show you how to create a habitat for your wild neighbors.

So you see, it's easy to help animals. And The HSUS is here to help.

2100 L Street NW • Washington, DC 20037 • 202-452-1100
www.hsus.org

Author Dedication

To Seth and Jordan,
as they find their way in and out of the virtual world

Trademark Disclaimer

Contents

Chapter 22: Internet   259

Chapter 23: Service Businesses   267

Chapter 24: Photography   277

Chapter 25: Special Events   **283**

Chapter 26: Writers   **291**

Chapter 27: Relocation and Real Estate Services   **299**

Chapter 28: Each Niche Stands Alone   **305**

Conclusion   **309**

Appendix: Sample Business Plan   **311**

Bibliography   **325**

Author Biography   **327**

Index   **329**

Foreword

Ten years ago, I decided to open my online business, New England Birdhouse, selling custom birdhouses that were replicas of my clients' homes. Armed with a unique niche product, knowledge of marketing, and stubborn persistence, I set out to stake my claim in the dot-com world.

After spending 20-plus years in the advertising industry, I recognized that I had a product perfectly suited to capitalize on the niche marketing potential of the Web, but no road map of how to build my online business — so I winged it. I surveyed the competition, brainstormed countless lists of domain names, wrote a lot of copy, and learned enough HTML code to cobble together my first Web site. Within a couple of months, I had my first custom birdhouse order; New England Birdhouse, at **www.newengland-birdhouse.com**, was officially in business.

Since that time, my Web site has been through countless design revisions. Search engine optimization (SEO), page rank, Facebook, and Twitter have become my recent online marketing obsessions. My Web site includes both a blog chock-full of original backyard birding articles, as well as a customer-service-supported online storefront selling birding supplies, garden and patio décor, and New England-style artisan wares. I maintain a waiting list for my custom birdhouses and have crafted them for clients across the United States and abroad.

At each step, I looked for a comprehensive guide that would help show me the way, and I believe that Sharon L. Cohen has finally written it.

For the entrepreneur on a shoestring, *199 Internet-Based Businesses You Can Start with Less than One Thousand Dollars: Secrets, Techniques, and Strategies Ordinary People Use Every Day to Make Millions* is not only a how-to guide to start an online business, but a must-have to thrive in the world of e-commerce. This helpful guide is for everyone who is exploring the possibility of starting an online business and for the seasoned online business owner who needs fresh marketing and advertising ideas to take a business to the next level.

The first chapter helps you through the process of determining whether being an online merchant is for you. Are you passionate about making this happen? Are you self-motivated? Do you have the commitment to stick to it through the ups and downs? What business skills do you bring to the table — are you organized, have a strong sense of customer service, or interested in marketing? Starting and building an online business is not easy, but it can be very rewarding.

Once you decide you're ready to make the jump, Cohen delivers a wealth of meaningful and current information, chapter by chapter. From organizing your office, to creating a Web site, to marketing your business, the book provides you with everything you need to consider.

Creating and building New England Birdhouse has taken me on a wonderful journey, filled with countless challenges and learning opportunities. Because the Internet is constantly evolving and improving, my path today is very different than it was ten years ago. If I were starting over, Cohen's book would be my first resource, as it is an invaluable and comprehensive step-by-step guide to being a successful online merchant.

Bill Askenburg, proprietor
New England Birdhouse
1-800-815-0062
www.newenglandbirdhouse.com
http://blog.NewEnglandBirdhouse.com

Birding enthusiast, woodworker, and stay-at-home dad Bill Askenburg created New England Birdhouse in 2001 to promote his custom architectural replica birdhouses; offer premium backyard birding supplies; and provide information and a connection for other birding enthusiasts. Using his 20-plus years of advertising experience, he designed and created his Web site and blog, featuring a catalog of premium birdhouses, bird feeders, garden décor, and uniquely New England artisan wares.

Introduction

The Arrival of the World Wide Web and E-Commerce

S hopping online for products and services is one of the most popular Web activities. It offers consumers a score of benefits, such as shopping at their own pace at any time, right from their desktop. There is no need to get dressed, drive in traffic, and fight the crowds in the mall, only to find out that the desired product is not available. According to Forrester Research, online retail sales for the United States hit $204 billion in 2008 and are forecasted to reach $335 billion by 2012.

If you want to become a part of this virtual world, this book will set you in the right direction. Before getting into the specifics of how you can establish one of these 199 businesses or another one of your own, let us review the history of the mainstay of your e-commerce venture — the Internet. By knowing how the online world has changed and how it continues to develop, you can start forming some of your own ideas about your online store.

Isn't it incredible to think that e-commerce only became possible in 1991 — so few years ago? Initially, the term e-commerce referred to the act of businesses exchanging financial data and conducting electronic transactions. Since then, hundreds of thousands of businesses and services, from the most general to the most specific, have made their home on the Web, and the term "e-commerce" means a great deal more.

The public started getting enthusiastic about Web commerce in the mid-1990s, but an important piece of the puzzle had to be completed in order to make newcomers more comfortable with online shopping. Several more years were needed to create security protocols, such as the Hypertext Transfer Protocol Secure, frequently used for Web payment transactions and exchanging confidential information online. At the turn of the 20th century, a large number of North American and European companies were already promoting their products and services on the Web, and e-commerce was being redefined. It meant that businesses and consumers were able to purchase available goods and services on the Internet with safe and secure payment vehicles, such as virtual shopping carts. The development of a secure payment gateway allowed merchants to safely accept credit cards and checks through electronic transmissions. It was a means for securely transacting sales, accepting returned merchandise, offering immediate authorizations, and screening for fraud. At the same time, virtual shopping carts allowed customers to buy more than one item at a time. When customers were finished shopping, their items were tallied. They could then accept the total amount and make an electronic payment, return any of the items in the cart, or leave the cart altogether.

Despite the dot-com crash in 2000, when many online ventures disappeared, many entrepreneurs and "brick-and-mortar" store owners could already see the potential of e-commerce. An increasing number of businesses began building their own Web sites with virtual shopping carts and secure electronic payment transactions. According to the U.S. Department of Commerce, retail e-commerce sales for the last quarter of 1999 were more than $5 billion, which rose to nearly $9 billion in 2000 and $10 billion in 2001. The estimate for total e-commerce sales for 2001 was nearly $33 billion, a 19 percent increase over 2000. This rise continued through the dot-com crash.

Online Shopping Models

It is impossible to discuss the history of the Web without looking at the extremely innovative business models established by online companies such as Amazon.com and eBay. Such innovations completely changed the way consumers viewed the Web's capabilities and its impact on their lives. To understand these revolutionary changes, compare what the Web was like when it was first established to what it has become today. You can equate this tremendous change to the arrival of the first American department stores. Imagine what it was like in the late 1800s when Macy's opened its doors in New York City. Buyers were used to small mom-and-pop stores. Here, instead, was a store occupying an entire city block with 9 floors, 33 elevators, and 4 escalators, and selling all the products one could imagine.

Now, jump ahead a century. Think about the millions of consumers in the mid-1990s who were used to going to traditional brick-and-mortar stores or buying from catalogs whenever they wanted a product. With Amazon's business model, these same buyers could turn on their computers and have the ultimate in convenience without ever leaving their home. They could peruse a wide selection of products — from books to electronics — directly from individual companies, with customer reviews and product descriptions provided to help them compare competing companies and make the best buying decision. Customers felt safe in making their financial transactions through virtual shopping carts, received numerous discount opportunities, and knew their product would be shipped within 48 hours. In addition, Amazon patented the "1-Click" buying system. This feature stored all buyers' payment information, so they could purchase their items with literally just one click of their mouse.

Amazon also introduced the affiliate marketing program, which continues to impact people like yourself who are seriously considering profiting from the world of e-commerce. Affiliate programs, which are now available with thousands of businesses, allow you to make money online by taking advantage of the marketing and branding of another company. With affiliate programs, you can make a commission by selling the products of another company on your own Web site. For example, when you become an affiliate of "Jones Dog Food Products" and begin to sell their items on your Web site, each time someone makes a purchase, you get a percentage of the sale. Keep in mind that you still have to do extensive marketing in order to let consumers know you have a Web site that sells Jones' products, but fortunately, all the product development, inventory tracking, and shipping is handled for you. In addition, numerous online sellers sell through the Amazon WebStore. With WebStore, you can have a Web site selling your own merchandise, but have it linked to Amazon's far-reaching marketing and sales distribution system. Whenever a consumer looks up products through Amazon.com, these Web stores get top billing. Amazon presently acquires approximately 40 percent of its sales from these affiliates and third-party sellers who list and sell goods on Amazon's Web site. When you establish your business, this is one of the avenues that you will want to seriously consider.

In 2008, approximately 615 million customers traveled to **www.amazon. com**, as reported by the Web analytics company **www.compete.com**. Besides the products themselves, customers appreciate the fact that Amazon offers a review system, giving users the ability to rate products, services, or companies from one to five stars.

Ebay is another company that has greatly increased the e-commerce consumer mindset. It is a win/win equation: Sellers can list items for sale, and buyers can bid on them. There is a separate category for each type of auction arranged by different topics of interest. Pierre Omidyar created eBay in his San Jose living room in 1995 so individuals could find a marketplace for the sale of goods and services. Ebay introduced a type of one-on-one online selling, which traditionally had been conducted through garage sales, collectible shows, and flea markets. With the eBay online auction and shopping Web site, people and businesses can bid on, buy, and sell a wide variety of goods and services from vendors worldwide. Buyers could quickly find their desired items, and sellers could register and start selling any items they had within minutes.

Ebay items are listed by categories, and account holders can bid on the item of their choice. Just about anything anyone can imagine — from the most common to the most rare — has been listed on eBay, such as electronics, automobiles, houses, antiques, concert tickets, CDs, DVDs, and artwork. In 2002, eBay acquired the online company PayPal, which allows merchants and consumers to safely buy and pay merchants through electronic payments via their e-mail address. PayPal money can be spent online through check or credit/debit cards to the account owner, or deposited into a bank account. If you are seriously considering starting your own online business, eBay has the largest online market for selling merchandise.

Dell is another company that has shaped the overall structure of the online experience. This leading computer company, headquartered in Texas, was launched in 1994, offering only one Web page of products. Within three years, it was boasting one million dollars in e-commerce sales. The company grew because it could sell goods over the Web without the costs associated with brick-and-mortar retail outlets and unnecessary middlemen. Dell could promote its products directly to the end users.

Since then, scores of online enterprises have followed this model. An important element in Dell's success is that it gives customers choice and control. People can build their own personal computers piece by piece, selectively choosing each necessary component depending on their budget and overall needs. Approximately 50 percent of the company's profits come from Web site sales. In 2007, Dell was listed as the 34th largest company in *Fortune* magazine's Fortune 500 list. Furthermore, according to *Fortune,* the company ranked eighth on the yearly "Top 20" list of the most successful and admired American companies due to the company's business model.

Demands of the Sophisticated Virtual Shopper

Today's online shopper is Web-savvy, which means online businesses must continually raise the bar and anticipate what customers will expect in the future. In the coming years, online consumers will want:

- Enhanced Web site accessibility and usability due to ever-expanding, new technologies.

- Greater multi-channel commerce choices, such as mobile devices, allowing Web stores to focus on personal relationships.

- More user-friendly and social e-commerce sites that expand community involvement and user input.

- Further reliance on retail Web sites that sell through catalogs.

- Increased use of analytics, allowing retailers to offer top-level customized service and competitiveness.

- Expanded ability of digital downloads that rely on newly developed software.

- More integration between virtual and brick-and-mortar shops, such as at-store product pickup.

- A larger number of global Web sites offering a variety of safe and secure payment options.

- Expanded marketing budgets for online promotions.

- Greater dependence on long-tail options, such as cataloging, allowing a smaller group or niche of customers to find small quantity or customized items. The "long tail" concept describes the niche strategy where businesses sell a large amount of specialized products, each in relatively small numbers.

- More emphasis on building brand over only selling products.

- Further expansion into new international markets to expand global presence.

- Greater reliance on other vendors who can offer the latest in payment provisions, such as Google Checkout™, where a consumer can conveniently buy from stores across the Web and track their orders and shipping information in one location.

- More personalization and community integration, where customers' habits are recognized and catered to.

The time has come when customers are no longer going online just because it is available. They want consistent, dependable, and easy-to-use service. To do so, retailers will need to continually test different methods and techniques and incorporate them into their online marketing initiatives. Web store owners must learn as much as possible about their potential customers in order to fulfill their particular shopping needs. When consumers have less discretionary funds, as in today's unstable economic market, they are more selective in their purchases. Online store owners need to be more innovative and put forth extra effort to distinguish themselves from the competition.

Before We Begin

In this book, you will find 199 different types of Web site businesses, and you can start for $1,000 or less. Here are some points to keep in mind.

1. The $1,000 does not include your computer, software, equipment, and office supplies.

2. It is assumed you will use a drop shipper, so you do not have to pay for the product until it is sold; or you are offering a service, so you do not need to pay for a product in advance; or you are selling some form of handmade item, and you buy materials but not the finished product.

3. Your cost for creating a Web site is included in this $1,000, so you need to find a company that offers a cost-effective rate for design and server. Another option is to design the Web site yourself.

4. Your cost for advertising is included in the $1,000. Therefore, you need to keep promotional costs low and do mostly organic, or do-it-yourself, marketing.

5. In the beginning, you will be working by yourself, or with a friend or relative, at either a low salary or free of charge. You have set aside some funds to keep you afloat for a minimum of three months.

6. The suggestions for businesses given here are just that: suggestions. You should use your own experience and expertise to decide what you want to sell or what services to provide.

This book is separated into two sections. The first section details everything you need to know about opening an e-commerce business. The last section lists 199 Internet businesses you can start for under $1,000. In the list of possible businesses, you will see three levels of possibilities. The first is the general category, such as "animals" or "advertising." This will direct you to the topic that best fits your expertise. Then, under this general topic, you will find some specific types of businesses. Third, for some businesses, you will see "sideline" businesses. Sidelines are spinoffs or niches of the other Web sites. They give you examples of how you can take a topic of interest and find you own unique opportunity in that industry. In Appendix A, you will find a sample business plan to help you format yours.

Section I:

Creating Your Business Model

Chapter 1

Is E-Commerce Right For You?

Traits of a Successful Business Owner

Individuals who start successful e-commerce businesses have certain traits in common. A successful business owner will be:

Passionate

Time and time again, e-commerce professionals tell beginners they must have a passion for the product or service they expect to sell. If these new Web site merchants expect to be successful, they must be willing to put in long hours and try as many different approaches as possible. After several months, their efforts will most likely begin to pay off. If you do not have a true interest in your business and a deep desire to watch your personal and financial investment progress, you will have a much more difficult time reaching success.

Committed

Before starting your business, you need to ask yourself some serious questions: In the past, when you have started other ventures, were you able to stay on point and see them through to the end? How about at your regular nine-to-five job? How was your performance record? When asked to do a job, even one you did not particularly like or enjoy, did you do your best anyway? This type of commitment is necessary. Be prepared for your life to be different once you launch your own Internet business. Talk with your close family members, so they know that your availability will be limited and that you might be more stressed than normal. Also, your personal life may not be as flexible as it has been in the past.

Forward-thinking

Because the Internet changes so quickly, you must be the type of person who continually looks for and recognizes opportunities when they present themselves, such as new forms of marketing. Some people are okay with the status quo and let others come up with the ideas and changes; then, they follow suit. Others see a headline in a magazine, such as "By 2015, the Internet will be the primary source of news for Americans," and suddenly start thinking about the impact it will make. You do not have to be a Thomas Edison or Benjamin Franklin and come up with new ideas. Yet, once you make the decision to begin your own online business, you need to be able to spot trends and predict the changes your business will need to make in the future to keep up with those trends. You constantly need to implement new techniques to promote your site and improve your processes to reach your store's maximum potential.

The Internet changes rapidly, so you always have to be on top of your game. You have to spend a great deal of time learning about online trends and talking with other people in the field, all while keeping your business afloat. Spend time searching the virtual world to see what is new. Read trade publications and journals related to Web retail and your industry. Keep up with trends, and always be aware of what other successful competitors are doing.

Original

It is not always necessary to wait for an idea or opportunity to present itself to you. Crazy, but lucrative, ideas — such as sites like **www.plentyoff-**

ish.com, www.gasbuddy.com, and **www.ratemyprofessors.com** — can come from anywhere, such as a book, a TV news program, or a comment you overhear. In most cases, these ideas are going to come when you least expect them. Successful e-commerce merchants try different approaches on their own. Originality also means continually searching for creative and different ways to solve new and existing problems, such as why customers are putting items in their shopping cart but not buying them, or why you are receiving multiple returns on a single item. You need to consider the problem from a completely unique perspective. This requires looking at an issue from all directions and always having an alternative method waiting in the wings. For instance, you may find a drop-ship company that always responds to your sales within 24 hours. What happens if this drop-ship company receives its product late from the manufacturer? You may have to make a decision right on the spot: Do you tell customers they have to wait longer for their purchases? Or, do you find another vendor, even if it means paying a premium price? Making such decisions before the problem arises might mean your customers would not have to suffer.

Originality also means venturing beyond your normal habits. Doing so is the only way your business will continue to expand and distinguish itself from the competition. For example, over the past few years, technology has begun to allow users to interact more with Web sites. Now with the use of this technology, users can design a variety of products from their homes. With a few clicks, they can design one-of-a-kind T-shirts, wedding invitations, birthday cakes, or shoes.

Motivated

With $1,000, an area of expertise or interest, and an idea that your research proves can be successful, anyone can open an online business in a matter of hours. That does not mean you are the right person to start an online business, nor that you would want to open a store without doing all the necessary prep work beforehand. You also must go into this venture with a strong "I can do it" mentality and an understanding that all businesses have risks. Know that only approximately 10 percent of online businesses succeed. Those that do not succeed have not put in enough time formulating a business plan with specific goals. When motivated, you are inspired to act on strategies and objectives. Personal motivation gets you up and moving every day. If you are going to have you own business, your boss, supervisor, or fellow workers will not be there to tell you to make phone calls or change product copy. Without personal motivation, it will be much more difficult to stay motivated and focused when the day does not go as planned. There are a large number of e-commerce merchants who quit before their business even has a chance of succeeding. Remember that sales will vary day to day. Some days there will be zero sales, and other days you will be swamped. The most successful e-commerce owners have enough personal motivation to find solutions to their problems.

Multi-talented

Running any kind of business also necessitates multi-tasking. You will be responsible for many different activities — especially if you are working alone. This may require you to order products from a drop-ship vendor through the phone, write new copy for the Web site or blog, examine the store's analytics, and package a product to send to a customer. As your business grows, you will be able to hire additional employees, but in the beginning, you will be responsible for all necessary tasks. Many e-commerce startups have only one or two people overseeing the planning, buying, sales, marketing, billing, and customer service. It is easy to get overwhelmed by the many ongoing duties involved in running the business, especially when the store is really busy. Your organization will greatly affect your ability to expand into new areas. You must maintain accurate records and an effective filing system that can adapt to changes with your business.

Available

You say you want to open an e-commerce business part-time or as a hobby. This is possible due to the flexibility of the Internet. When you have a brick-and-mortar store, you have to literally open the doors every day at scheduled hours. Online, it does not matter when you open; however, you must be capable of servicing customers worldwide, all day and night. Even if you plan on operating part-time, you must give customers the means for using your store around the clock. On your Web site, provide customers with the hours when an actual person — you — will be available to answer questions. Remember: What you get out of this venture depends on what you put into it. If you only work a few hours each day, it will take you much longer to grow your business. If you only work part-time, you need to be even more precise on how you will spend each hour. It is necessary to make a list of priorities each day, so you will not be tempted to turn your attention to other business activities.

Business-oriented

Although it is helpful to have business skills when starting your e-commerce store, it is not completely essential. Many skills will be learned as you gain experience, or you can take a quick business course through community college, adult education, or distance learning before starting. Instead of becoming a business genius, focus on thinking clearly, logically, and inventively, and emphasize having strong management and organizational skills. You must spend time and money on advertising to market your Web site and products. Naturally, it is helpful to have a strong sense of customer service, facility with basic mathematics and accounting skills, interest in marketing, and ability for recordkeeping. An interest and ability in Internet technology is important as well.

Committed to continued education

While operating your own online store, you will learn a great deal of new information needed to be a successful online merchant. You will discover you are the one who continually must make decisions. When inventory needs to be found, taxes must be paid, ads have to be written and posted, and the Web site has to be redesigned, you are the one who will be responsible. If you already have an established brick-and-mortar business, these may not be new skills, but rest assured, there will be a host of new areas you will add to your repertoire. You should never stop learning. The online world is always changing, and you must do the same.

Practical

There is a danger that many new merchants encounter that keeps them from attaining a successful business: a belief that an online business is an easy way to make money without doing much work. Do not fool yourself into believing that starting an online business is any easier or any less demanding than it would be to open a traditional brick-and-mortar operation. Far too often, individuals start an online store because they truly feel it will make them wealthier and require much less work than an offline business. You need to be practical about the requirements of an e-commerce business and what you will gain — or not gain — by the degree of your participation. Making a place for yourself in a particular niche requires a lot of work. It will not happen overnight. You can expect to wait several months before you see results. You will not make millions on your first attempt at starting an e-commerce store.

Brick-and-Mortar versus Online Store

Why would you want to start an online business rather than a traditional brick-and-mortar business? Here are some of the differences between the two that will help you answer this question:

- **"Please touch"**: Customers who visit brick-and-mortar stores can actually see the product in person, pick it up, or touch all the parts. Online stores can only upload products photos and descriptions. Many customers have difficulty making a decision from a photograph. As described in a case study in this book, an online kitchen cabinet business actually sends a sample of the wood and its color to customers to help them choose to help combat this issue.

- **Cutting costs**: Normally, starting a physical store is quite a hefty financial undertaking. There are costs associated with rental of store space, utilities, employees, maintenance, and a host of other necessities. With an online business, there are very few start-up costs — beyond the cost of the server. You do not, for example, need to be concerned with signing a lease or paying for heat.

- **Worldwide 24/7**: With a brick-and-mortar store, you will not be open all day every day. Similarly, unless you have catalogs that are sent all over the world, you will most likely be servicing only local customers and clients. E-commerce merchants sell throughout the globe from their primary location, no matter where it is. Many customers can shop at the same time without the fear of crowds, and they can do it any time of the day.

- **Face-to-face:** Customer communication is essential, as is personalized attention. This can be achieved more effectively in a traditional store when the owner and customer are face to face. It is often difficult to interact with customers online. It is necessary to establish a variety of different ways to communicate with customers, such as e-mails, e-zines, online chats, and forums. Also, it should be easy for customers to find answers to their questions, access certain information, such as the catalog, and perform operations, such as using the shopping cart.

- **Work full- and part-time**: Due to the flexibility of Internet-based businesses, it is possible to start and build your business while still having full-time employment elsewhere. You can simply devote time during the evenings and on weekends, or whenever you have free time, to building your business. Because an Internet-based business allows you to work around your day job, you are able to maintain a full-time income while your e-business is still young. Owning a brick-and-mortar business does not allow for this type of flexibility; it is usually all-or-nothing.

- **Greater expectations**: Online customers are more spoiled than those who generally shop at brick-and-mortar stores. They have high customer service expectations. They want to easily be able to search and find the product, find a clear product description, and conduct their transactions — whether it is with a shopping cart, through PayPal, or by making a telephone call. If they cannot get the product they want — for the price they want to pay and when they want it — online customers will quickly leave your site and go somewhere else.

The Niche Reigns Supreme

A niche market can be defined as a targeted group of people with similar and very specific needs or interests. These individuals participate in the same activities and, therefore, will most likely want the same goods or services. When the Internet first started, e-commerce consisted of many superstores, such as Amazon, which sell a wide range of items. In most cases, those days are over. Now, businesspeople become successful by selling a product line that is of interest to a small niche of people whose buying needs have yet to be met by a current merchant. The new merchant builds a community of loyal customers who return to the Web site often for information and entertainment, as well as to purchase additional items.

Because marketing to a niche market is important for building a successful business, you should not finalize your products or services until you have selected your niche and determined their specific requirements. Internet professionals warn that the majority of online stores do not succeed because owners first selected the product to be sold and then looked for the market that would buy it. In many of these cases, the product demand is not large enough to support a business, and the competition is too strong. Go into any sports store, and you will see shoes for every sport imaginable. These products were made after recognizing the niche and then filling the need of individuals participating in this sport. The following are a few steps to consider for selecting your niche product or service line.

1. Sit down with a notepad and begin to think of all the niches that can fall within your area of expertise, experience, and interest. You will have great difficulty promoting products that you do not know or care about. The consumers will see through you in a second if they are passionate about the topic.

2. Look at each of those niches and start your research, including potential buyers, demand for the product or service, and merchandise having the greatest possibility for sales. You can determine the popularity of a niche by using Google or Yahoo! keyword services to gauge how often people have searched for certain terms during a given time. For example, using Google, type keywords, such as "green baby products," and Google will return a list of other similar keywords and display how many people have recently searched for those keywords. In October 2009, 1,300 people searched for the keyword "green baby products" on Google. However, 9,900 searched for "organic baby products," 2,900 searched for "organic cotton baby clothes," and 18,100 for "organic baby clothes." You can determine how much traffic your Web site will receive based on the keywords you use.

3. Another way to discover new trends related to your business is to join online discussion groups, such as forums or newsgroups, and

carefully read the comments. For example, in many of the moms-to-be or new mom forums, the members may write something like, "I'm looking for earth-friendly organic baby products, but they are all so expensive. Does anyone know of a Web site that is more reasonable?" or "I'm looking for all-natural shampoo for my baby. Any suggestions?" After visiting these forums frequently, you will begin to notice a trend relating to the most requested products. If you need advice regarding your business or Web site, do not be afraid to ask the members what they would be interested in seeing.

4. When you have decided on a niche, find out more about the competition. Some competition is important. It is much more difficult to start a Web business when a niche is too specific and there are no other sites offering similar products or services, as you will have a great deal more marketing to do. On the other hand, you do not want thousands of competitors. If there is a handful of substantial competitors, you are on the way to developing your new business. If there are a number of strong players in the game, you need to create a unique way to differentiate your products or services from these competitors, or you can find a more specific offshoot of your niche market. For example, suppose you want to develop a business selling dog bones, but upon your research, you discover there are countless Web sites that sell dog bones. A narrower niche would include natural health bones or dog bone gift baskets. By choosing this route, your competitors are no longer those selling all types of dog bones, but rather those who sell natural dog bones.

5. After deciding on a niche product or service, begin by selling just a few of the items of interest to this specialized audience. Begin with those products your research has found to be the most popular. Because you should already have established a relationship with members of a few forums and discussion boards, run your products

by them. Ask for comments. If your research is accurate, you will be meeting a need and will, most likely, receive a good response.

6. Most importantly, it is necessary to establish yourself and your site as the best Internet resource serving this niche. Your Web site should contain articles, guides, instructions, customer product reviews, your personal comments about products, and comments from customers in order to offer the most pertinent information. For example, going back to the example of the natural dog bone Web site, you could write an e-book on nutrition for canines. First, you establish your expertise, and then, when you gain a following, you expand your product line with customer recommendations. Eventually, you may sell products related to this niche, such as dog vitamins, or start an entirely different site to sell to another niche. Selecting a niche establishes the foundation of your business and determines how it will grow in the months and years to come. Thus, you should spend considerable time defining your specialized product. Do not try to rush through or ignore this step, automatically assuming you have an ingenious idea. You can be up and running and then fail very quickly if you are not satisfying a particular need.

Most towns have a convenience or general store selling a variety of items. However, the store will only sell the products most in demand because of the limited shelf space. If you are interested in organic, whole-wheat noodles, for example, you are not going to find them at a general store. Smaller stores cannot use their limited space to stock a large variety of items that only a small number of people want; if they did, these products would stay on the shelves for months. They can only carry products that are going to sell most often.

But e-commerce merchants do not have such limitations. They can offer hundreds of specialized models of a particular item because they are not concerned with limited shelf space. E-commerce merchants have an unlimited amount of *virtual* shelf space on their Web sites. Increasingly, online businesses are not stocking physical inventory (as would a brick-and-mortar store). Instead, they are using drop-ship services or drop shippers to deliver their goods to customers. Drop shippers are manufacturers and/or suppliers who store products for their online customers in an off-site location until the products are ordered. When the retailer notifies the drop shipper that a sale has been made, the drop shipper automatically ships the product to the retailer's customer and handles payment administration. Because the retailer does not have to be concerned about inventory costs and shipping, it is much easier to respond to a niche market. There are many drop shippers from which to choose. Do not go with any firm that requests a monthly fee for its services. You should not need to pay for anything except the product and shipping.

Because e-commerce merchants have so many options when it comes to inventory and shipping, the product niche can be as specific as merchants choose. There are e-commerce stores selling nothing but a single line of baby car seats, antique Mustang parts, or adhesive tape. Can you imagine opening up a traditional brick-and-mortar store selling only adhesive tape? It is very possible online. The large multi-product Web stores can no longer run the show as they have in the past. Today, even a small niche Web site can compete with the big guys — and succeed. There are millions of small markets waiting to be served, and you can be the one to serve them.

Chapter 2

Benefits of an Online Business

Today, offline businesses and entrepreneurs can readily see the benefits that e-commerce offers. Potential customers from all over the world can quickly search Web site catalogs and find their desired products and services. For example, on **www.Shopper.com** — an online Web site catalog — customers can "find the right product at the right price." Shopper.com provides an extensive catalog with thousands of user and professional product reviews, comparison specifics, and product prices for computers and consumer electronics.

With online Web site catalogs, consumers can view and compare numerous products, contemplate the purchase, then return to the site when they are ready to buy. Then, with a click of the mouse, their items drop into their shopping cart, and they are out the virtual door.

In addition, search engine technology helps customers easily find items of interest. The Yellow Pages are nothing compared to complex search engines, such as Google, Bing, and Yahoo!. A consumer searching for a product does not even need to input the exact word into the search engine. Even a description or a question will bring correct results, as search engines like Google use an algorithm to sort information to mimic human thought. When someone conducts a search, Google supplies information on the keyword frequency and location within the Web page. If the keyword only appears once on the site, the site will receive a low keyword score, thus appearing farther down in the search engine's results. Web sites with a high keyword score will appear farther up on the results page. Google also allows the searcher to know the length of time the Web page has been available. Pages with a long and established history are valued more, thus being more likely to be near the top of the search engine's results page. In order to receive a higher ranking on Google or other search engines, business owners must spend considerable time marketing their Web site. Yet, with online marketing, they will not have the high advertising costs associated with offline marketing. With a much more level playing field, smaller companies — such as yourself — can market to the same global customer base as the largest e-commerce businesses.

E-commerce continues to evolve into new virtual worlds, with the priority of meeting the customers' specialized needs. Online stores are evolving from quantity- to quality-based selling, especially as they extend their reach worldwide. It no longer matters where an e-commerce shop is located — in a European city with millions of people, a small town in China, or a garage in midwestern America. In order to open for business, grow, and continue to survive, a Web store must quickly adapt to changing circumstances. Merchants must increase and change their product line while making sure that these items are easy-to-use, attractive, cost-competitive, modern with state-of-the-art technology standards, and fulfilling for the needs of customers as advertised.

There are Many Opportunities Available

Using the Internet, you can start any business you desire, as long as there are at least a few people interested in the product you are selling. Plus, there are a variety of ways to make money on the Web beyond operating your own retail or service store, including using affiliate advertising, developing an income-generating blog, or selling products on a site such as Amazon or eBay. Information is very important to most online users. In fact, in many cases, they will make their decision on where to buy their products based on the credibility of informed sources. Rather than actually selling a product or service, some people write informative blogs on a specific topic. In their articles and on their blog site, they recommend e-commerce sites and receive a commission for lead generation or sales.

E-Commerce is Inexpensive

Developing a Web site or blog is a low-cost option compared to opening up a store or office. Even if designing your own Web site is not among your abilities, you can find templates to get you started for free, or for a very low price. Paying for a domain name is inexpensive, as low as $10.00 for a year with companies such as GoDaddy, Google Apps, Immotion, Yahoo!, and Super Green. The cost of Web hosting will vary. A Web hosting company retains the pages of your Web site on a server, which is software and hardware that stores and processes large amounts of data. While your business is new and the sales volume is low, you can find a Web host for $10 to $20 per month, or choose a company offering hosting in conjunction with domain name registration. With Homestead, Intuit's simple Web site design program, customers pay as low as $4.99 to use one of the company's 2,000 templates to create and publish a Web site. Or, you can pay a bit more and get additional services from Homestead, such as search engine optimization to achieve higher search engine rankings. However, as business increases, you will need to have more technical capability and assistance, and this leads to paying more for your Web site. In addition, as your sales increase and your business grows, you will also need to expand your marketing efforts. An online business saves money due to the lack of overhead expenses, such as electricity and rent — yet you continue to have other costs, such as advertising. To decrease inventory costs, you should consider manufacturing your own product, providing a service rather than a product, or purchasing drop-shipped items.

E-commerce Continues to Expand

Although some brick-and-mortar stores have succumbed to economic pressures and the rise of Internet business, e-commerce continues to expand. An estimated 627,200 new brick-and-mortar employer firms began operations in 2008, and 595,600 firms closed that year. This amounts to an annual turnover of about 10 percent for entry and 10 percent for exit. Non-employer firms — businesses that do not employ workers — have turnover rates three times as high as those of employer firms, mostly because of easier entry and exit conditions. Cyber stores do not have to pay high rent payments, so they can cut the price of their products as much as 40 percent. In addition, in a shaky economy, consumers are more attracted to shopping online, rather than driving from store to store, scoping out bargains. Shoppers like the convenience of online shopping. The Web does somewhat feel the impact, however, as economists say high-end and some middle-end e-commerce products do not do as well as other middle-end and low-end products. In a survey by Forrester Research, Inc. (**www.forrester.com**), 19 percent of consumers said they plan to spend more on the Web in 2009 than 2008. U.S. non-travel e-commerce sales grew by 13 percent from 2007 to 2008 and are forecast to increase 11 percent in 2009. These figures do show a significant slowdown from 2007, when Internet sales increased 18 percent more than the previous year. Much of this slowing down is due to consumer confidence, which impacted e-commerce sales for much of 2009. Regardless, Web sales are expected to be positive as e-commerce continues to take market share from brick-and-mortar stores.

Marketing and Advertising Online is Cost-Effective

Marketing consists of activities and processes for creating, communicating, delivering, and exchanging information on what an organization can offer its customers or clients in comparison to the competition. Marketing is crucial to all businesses, and you do not necessarily have to pay for it. With Internet marketing, it is possible to devote just time and effort — rather than money — and achieve positive results. Plus, with Internet marketing, you can advertise your product or service to the whole world with only a few clicks of your mouse. According to Internet World Stats (**www.internetworldstats.com**), there are approximately 1.6 billion Internet users worldwide as of mid-2009 — equal to 25 percent of the Earth's population. The number of people online increased more than 300 percent between 2000 and 2008, and this growth is forecasted to continue as the Internet becomes more widespread across Africa, China, and the Middle East.

A 2008 survey conducted by Hearst Electronics Group found that nearly half of all marketing-related expenses, or 47 percent, is spent online. Businesses realize that with the help of Internet technology, it is easier to sell, track their marketing impact, and make follow-up decisions in the virtual world. It is even possible to immediately see how a change on a Web site will affect a customer's buying habits. The cost of advertising on the Internet can be kept quite low compared to offline marketing. Admittedly, Internet marketing becomes more complex each year as Google and other search engines change the way they rank Web sites. A commitment to continual training is required to keep up with new trends.

Real-Time Customer Tracking with Analytics

It is critical for Web site owners to know the number of visitors to their site, how visitors found their site, how long visitors stayed, and what visitors did while there. All these questions are answered with Web site analytics. All Web servers, or the software and hardware maintaining the sites, keep activity logs. None of this information is easy to ascertain. For example, if you want to know the number of visitors at any given time, you need to look at statistics, such as the number of "hits." You would determine this number by analyzing all of the following information: the number of people requesting information on your Web site, the number of pages those people viewed, the number of different times one person visited your site, and the number of different or "unique" visitors visiting the site. "A million hits" does not mean much. Instead, it is important to report, "In 45,000 page views, there were over 15,000 visitor sessions with 10,000 unique visitors." The information becomes even more complex when considering what Web page a user was at before coming to your site — whether it was a search engine, another Web site, or blog — what keywords were searched, and what browser, Internet address, or company the visitor is affiliated with.

Online technology continues to become increasingly sophisticated. For example, Google Analytics is a free service provided by Google that offers you detailed statistics on consumers who are visiting your Web site. With Google Analytics, you can find out information such as the keywords people used to find your site, how long they stayed on your site, and aspects of your site that may be driving customers away — or keeping them on your pages longer.

In 2008, a considerably tough economic year, Americans continued to use the Internet for clothing, electronic, and even automobile purchases. 125 retailers were interviewed for *The State of Retailing Online 2008*, the 11th annual Shop.org study by Forrester Research, Inc. These Internet retailers' sales climbed 17 percent to $204 billion for the year. Excluding travel purchases, which ranked first, apparel led at $27 billion in sales, followed by computers at $24 billion, and cars at $19 billion. The strength of e-commerce was demonstrated by the fact that sales rose so significantly despite the economic situation worldwide.

Store owners spend a great deal of time looking for online trends and the impact they have on marketing. They are always trying to find new ways to attract customers and to retain original ones. For example, search engine optimization (SEO) allows you to achieve higher search engine rankings by using specific keywords in your Web site name, product descriptions, and body copy. The more your keywords correspond to searchers' requests, the better you will rank on the search engines. However, online stores have not stopped their offline marketing efforts. They continue to draw customers online with traditional marketing efforts, such as catalogs and advertisements. At the same time, these merchants are always trying out new promotional approaches. In the past, they found they could increase sales with free shipping. Now, more retailers are increasing customer numbers and establishing their image by focusing on newer marketing vehicles such as social media networking and widgets. When a member of a social media site, such as Facebook or LinkedIn, enjoys your blog or e-commerce site, he or she may share it with their online friends. These people will tell their friends, and soon, this information distributed to hundreds of thousands of visitors. When you promote your Web business with social media marketing, your Web site's content is critical; the more thorough and informative it is, the more likely it will be passed from one person to the next. Widgets, which are noted by small icons, are little snippets of HTML code embedded on Web site pages, blogs, and social network sites. Once you clearly define your customers' needs and wants, you can use widgets to enhance their experience. For example, widgets can include podcasts, videos, calendars, references, and games. People may end up interacting with this widget several times a week.

Customer reviews are another tool that online businesses are using as a marketing tool. In the past, only companies selling large volumes of product used these reviews, such as Amazon, but now customers expect to see reviews as a regular feature on all Web sites offering merchandise.

Marketers have been interested in analytics since the Web's beginning, and many companies offer different versions. In order to be competitive in this market, Google acquired Urchin, a Web site analytics company, in 2005, renamed it Google Analytics, and has since grown this end of the business. The search engine promises, "Google Analytics tells you everything you want to know about how your visitors found you and how they interact with your site. Focus your marketing resources on campaigns and initiatives that deliver a large return on investment (ROI), and improve your site to convert more visitors." Google Analytics gives you the opportunity to track a customer's online activity once visiting your e-commerce site, letting you to track why a sale is — or is not — made. Keeping track of how your business is doing on a continual basis is important, regardless of what type of products or services you sell. It is important to know if you are putting your time, effort, and money where it will have the most impact on sales. If visitors are coming to your Web site and then leaving right away, or they are putting products in their shopping cart and then never buying them, you are doing something incorrectly. There may be an unappealing or uncomfortable aspect to your site driving them away. Often, it can be something trivial, such as the color of the page or a certain technique involved with the shopping cart system. For example, suppose a company decided to make changes to the design of its Web site and wanted to measure the reaction of visitors during the transition. One of the minor changes the company decided to make was making one link red instead of blue in order to encourage more clicks on a coupon. A week later, when looking at Google Analytics, the company had a 65 percent jump in the number of clicks on that link. This is an example of how analytics can be used to determine whether customers like the design of your company's Web site.

The Ability to Follow Your Interests

Starting an e-business allows for a lot of flexibility, especially if you operate it part-time or for extra income. Whatever your interest, from collecting bottle caps to selling online avatar clothing, you can start a Web site. In many cases, it is not so much what is being sold as who is doing the selling. Your visitors will keep coming back if they feel part of a community and appreciate your expertise. Even if you are working full-time, this can be an enjoyable hobby that brings in additional income. You will make new contacts and friends in your field of interest and be able to share information with them. By operating an e-business, you may hear about conferences or social get-togethers with other people who share your interest. The following are a breakdown of the plusses and minuses to owning an e-commerce business over a traditional brick-and-mortar business.

E-commerce pros:

- Lower start-up costs and overhead

- Worldwide online presence

- Open for business all day, every day

- Work from home or remotely

- Opportunity to reach millions of new customers

E-commerce cons:

- No storefront visibility

- Not seeing customers

- Constant update of Web site

- Long days, nights, and hours

- Customer leeriness about business safety

- Possible crossover between business and family

Chapter 3

Organizing Your Office and Developing a Budget

Firewall: A computer system function that blocks or prevents unwanted intrusions into your computer. It allows you to perform legitimate functions while preventing adverse entries into your computer.

Anti-spam: A software program that allows you to prevent unwanted solicitations, such as e-mail advertisements, from ever making it into your inbox. You can download or purchase such a program, and the unwanted e-mail — or most of it — will be directly routed into your junk or trash folder.

Anti-virus: A software program that can be used to block harmful problems in your computer. The software can be set to scan your computer and seek out such harmful viruses and block or disable them. Or, it can be used to remove such viruses that may have found their way into your computer

Security settings: Various measures you can take to increase the security level on your computer. Your security settings can usually be found at the top of your home page, under the Tools section.

Learn the Lingo	**Temporary files, cookies:** Files that save or store information about sites you visit during your time browsing the Internet.

One of the myriad of tasks involved with starting an e-business is setting up your office. You want to have everything in place and ready to go before you actually "open your store" for business. You will have enough to keep you busy in the first months, and you do not want to worry about buying furniture or looking for equipment. You need to decide whether you will be working from home or renting an office space, what equipment and supplies you need, and how to design your workspace so it is comfortable and efficient.

An important question to consider at this point is where your business office will be located. Are you going to work from home or rent an office? Online merchants do either, depending on their needs. Some like to work from an office located in their home because it saves money, allows them to be near their children, and offers easy access to the computer and phone. If you decide to work from home, it is important to be secluded from other activities within the house. Once you begin working, then unless an emergency arises, interruptions should be avoided as much as possible. This practice allows for superior customer service and a more work-oriented environment. Often, people who plan for this arrangement actually have more family time because it allows them to get all their work done in a specified time period. It is important to establish this practice from the beginning with the other family members, as working from your home can become difficult if there is no separation between work and play. Online merchants who work from a different location like the routine of getting out of the house, socializing with other people, and separating from the computer at night.

Whether you work from home or a separate office location also depends on the type of online business you will operate. If you are selling a product that will be drop shipped, you can work anywhere. If you are making your own products, you need extra space. Or, if you have a Web site that supports a service, you may actually have a brick-and-mortar business as well as the online presence.

Electronics and Software

A reliable computer will be your most important piece of equipment because it is your gateway to your Web site. It is necessary to have a computer that facilitates your business needs, but this does not mean you necessarily need a high-end computer, especially if you are attempting to keep startup expenses as low as possible. If you have not purchased a new computer recently, you may be surprised by the fact that you can get a decent computer at a very low price. The most important issue is reliability. The computer must be operational whenever you need it. When your computer crashes, you will be unable to access your Web site and fill customer needs. Therefore, if you have an older, unreliable computer, it may be time to purchase a new one in order to build a thriving business.

If your older computer has truly been a trusty workhorse, have a computer specialist evaluate its performance capabilities to ensure it is capable of handling the tasks necessary for your business. You may be able to upgrade your present computer to add needed capabilities. Before doing this, compare the cost of upgrading your present computer with purchasing a new system. If you are starting a part-time e-business or looking for supplemental income, you may be able to use an older computer or one at the local library. This will require you to establish a specific schedule and rely on another facility's capability.

To find a computer that matches your needs, read computer magazines, such as *Website Magazine* and *Entrepreneur Magazine* (both are in print and online), and visit Web sites that rate the various brand names, such as Consumer Search (**www.consumersearch.com**) and All Business (**www. allbusiness.com**). Remember to pay attention to the brand's reputation for reliability. Make a checklist of the computer capabilities most important to your line of work to help you narrow down your choices. The computer will be your connection to the Internet and, ultimately, your customers. Processor speeds, the size of the hard drive, and the operating systems will be of interest to you. Below are some of the basics that you should be considering when setting up your online business office.

Processor (CPU)

The CPU, or the central processing unit, is often called the computer's "brain" because it runs the whole computer. When software is operating on your computer, the CPU completes all the program commands. The greater the CPU speed, the faster the computer will typically load programs. Speed is measured in MHz (megahertz) or GHz (gigahertz).

Hard drive

All computers have a hard drive, or an area that stores all permanent data, including operations, programs, and user files. Hard drive storage area is measured in bytes, with the typical capacities stated in KB (kilobytes), MB (megabytes), GB (gigabytes), and even TB (terabytes). Your existing desktop computer can be upgraded to include a second hard drive for additional storage. Although installing an additional hard drive on your computer is not a difficult task, you should consult with a computer professional at your local electronics store to find out if your system can be upgraded. Another option available is purchasing an external hard drive. External hard drives are not installed into the body of your computer and are, instead, connected to your computer's universal serial bus (USB) port. They offer the same amount of storage space as an internal hard drive and are an excellent option for backing up important data on your computer. External hard drives can be purchased at your local electronic store.

Backing up your data should be a top priority, and something you should do daily. Backing up data consists of copying files or databases so they will be saved in another location (such as an external hard drive or DVD discs) in case of an equipment failure. Backing up business data should be a part of your usual business routine, so setting a schedule for backing up data is important. For personal computer users, backing up is necessary but often neglected. The retrieval of files you have previously backed up is called "restoring" them. But a virus or hard drive failure could completely wipe out your computer. Backup drives connect to your computer through a USB, and you can choose from a variety of different drives, such as removable media (an external hard drive), memory cards with readers, and flash drives. Increasingly, people are purchasing small USB units that have a storage space of 1GB or more and can be placed on a key ring, or worn around the neck. Some backup drives include software that backs data up at assigned times. Because many people often forget to back up their data, there are many companies available that offer automatic, off-site back-up services such as **www.mozy.com** and **www.remotedatabackups.com**.

Memory

"Memory" and "hard drive space" are two different entities. As noted, hard drive space refers to the available amount of storage capacity on the computer's hard disk(s). Memory, instead, refers to the amount of random access memory (RAM) installed in the computer. RAM allows for stored data on the computer to be accessed in any order (thus, random). Another key difference between hard drive space and memory is that the data on a hard disk is not lost when the computer is turned off. In comparison, any information in memory is gone when you shut down your computer. RAM is usually expressed in megabytes or gigabytes. Your desktop computer can be upgraded to include additional RAM. In fact, when a computer is upgraded, adding additional RAM is usually one of the first upgrades made. In a sense, the more RAM your computer has, the faster it will be able to access stored data, thus making your computer run faster. Again, RAM is not difficult to install, but it must be installed correctly in order for your computer to run. Consult with a computer professional for help with upgrading your computer.

Total unit recommendations

You will want a desktop computer with at least 2GB of RAM and a hard drive with 250GB for low-end work to 500GB for high-end, and a processor at the speed of 2GHz. The default graphics card should be adequate unless you plan to design your own Web site or are handling graphics. You should speak with a computer professional regarding the operating system and processor best suited to your needs. When purchasing a new computer, get a one-year warranty with toll-free support. Because you may be working at odd hours, you should be able to reach customer support 24 hours a day, even on the weekends.

Digital camera

With a digital camera, you can take pictures of your products and upload them to your Web site. This will allow customers to view a photo of the product they intend to purchase. It is important to have a camera that produces crisp, high-resolution images and is simple to operate.

High megapixel capacity

If you try to enlarge images taken with a low-resolution camera to a size larger than 400 x 600 pixels, you will quickly see that the camera takes poor-quality photos. Pixels, short for picture element, are very small dots that make up an image on a computer display. The image is made up of hundreds of thousands, and sometimes millions, of these tiny pixels. "Resolution" is the image these pixels create. With a low-resolution camera, you will actually see pixels on the image. This makes the picture appear grainy.

With online photos, you need a camera with a high resolution. To create accurate, detailed images of your products that can be enlarged to 800 x 1,200 pixels or larger, you will need a digital camera with no less than a 6-megapixel capacity. Cameras are now available with up to a 12.1-megapixel capacity, which can produce images that can be used not only in online marketing, but also in fliers and posters for offline marketing.

Optical zoom

Nearly every digital camera has a zoom feature allowing you take close-up shots without moving closer to the subject you are photographing. When shopping for a digital camera, it is important to note whether a particular model features *optical* or *digital* zoom. Digital zoom enlarges a portion of the image simulating optical zoom; that is, the camera crops a part of the image and then enlarges it back to size. When it does this, the image quality is lost. It can cause the same sort of pixelation that occurs when you enlarge a low-resolution image on your computer. Optical zoom, on the other hand, works by physically distancing the lenses within the camera, much like a traditional 35mm film camera. This allows you to create a close-up image that is undistorted and free from the pixelation caused by a digital zoom.

Video camera

In recent years, videos of products have emerged as a hot Internet-marketing trend. People love to watch videos, and it has become quite easy to upload files from a video camera to a computer and embed them on your Web site. For example, someone who sells natural yarns may want to include a video on their Web site showing how the yarn was handmade on a spinning wheel. Although embedded video is by no means a required element, it is an excellent way to keep your Web site visitors around longer so they will be more likely to purchase from you. You will need a Web-optimized camcorder — a camcorder that has specialized features like built-in software that enables you to directly upload your videos. They can shoot video in standard definition of 640 x 480 pixels, or high definition of 720p or 1280p. Because they are small, however, you need a steady hand or a tripod to keep from blurring the visual. Sony, Samsung, Kodak, and RCA make models perfect for marketing purposes. Also, digital camcorders are often cameras as well, so there is no need to purchase both.

Phone and Internet service

For IRS tax purposes, business credibility, and privacy needs, consider dedicating a phone line to your business. Having a separate phone number also increases customer satisfaction, giving customers a number they can reach you at directly. You can get an Internet-based phone — through companies such as Vonage — or a traditional phone line for a low monthly price. Many businesses also use cell phones as their primary number, but it is important to make sure you have clear service within your home before deciding to use a cell phone as your main source of business communication. You do not want to be in the middle of a conversation with a customer and have your phone drop the call. You have several options for a means to receive phone messages from customers, such as a traditional answering machine, voicemail, or an answering service. Also consider whether you want to pay extra for a toll-free number.

With bundled services, you can choose from cable and phone service packages. Every bundled package consists of telephone, TV, and Internet service. Through a telephone company, you will receive satellite TV, telephone, DSL (digital subscriber loop) Internet — which provides Internet service over the telephone line instead of through a cable connection — and perhaps cellular service. A cable company will provide you with cable TV, cable Internet, and digital phone service. You may not need the TV in your bundle right now; however, as the Internet and television become more closely aligned — for example, being able to view incoming e-mails while watching TV or using your TV to access the Internet — you may want to consider this. The most important aspect of these services is the Internet connection. A reliable Internet connection is paramount. Internet service providers (ISPs) offer packages to meet your needs with prices that vary depending on the type and speed of the connection you choose.

As a business owner, you will need a broadband or high-speed cable Internet connection. This type of connection transmits data through a cable line and is capable of transmitting data approximately 50 to 100 times faster than a dial-up connection. An added advantage of a high-speed Internet connection is because it does not use a telephone line to access the Internet, your phone line will be free while you are online. A new AT&T DSL service, however, offers a connection that is just as fast as cable. A DSL connection is usually less expensive, so consider this to keep your expenses low when first starting your business.

Wireless Internet

Flexibility is one of the benefits of an owning an online business. Consider using a laptop with a built-in wireless card for wireless (Wi-Fi) capabilities. Wi-Fi service allows you to connect to the Internet at locations away from your home. Having a wireless card installed in your laptop will allow you to access the Internet on the go in designated Wi-Fi locations (such as your local coffee shop or bookstore). Most new computers automatically come with wireless cards built into the system. At home, you will need to buy an Internet router to wirelessly access the Internet. This will allow you to access the Internet from anywhere within your home, including in bed or out by the pool. This is a perfect option for people who have other responsibilities around the home during work hours, allowing you to not be confined to a desk.

Creating a Budget

When establishing a budget for your new business, recognize that it is a projection of income and expenses over time. As you start out, it is helpful to budget for at least a year, perhaps two or three. Begin by outlining each of your expenses (overhead, staffing, Web site maintenance, inventory, and insurance, for example) for the time period selected. You should also allow for unexpected expenses in your monthly budget, which will also help ward off excess stress. When first starting a business, unexpected expenses are a fact of life, so a small slush fund is always helpful. Then, project your income for the same period. Remember, in the first few months — even up to a couple of years — your business may not turn a profit.

For the purposes of this book, we will assume your budget to be $1,000. To accomplish this, it will be necessary to keep your overhead costs as low as possible. This may mean establishing a home office or working out of your garage or basement. Or, if you already have a brick-and-mortar store, set aside an area for this business. You may be unable to purchase new equipment, so look for used or rented equipment you can use during this time. Due to capping start-up expenses at $1,000, you will need to determine which items are most necessary now and which can be bought as your business begins to develop.

Next, list the income you expect to make for the period. In the beginning, this estimate should be conservative. The first few months will likely be slow, especially as it takes several months for marketing efforts to prove effective. Compare your income to necessary expenses. Do the numbers equal? Are you making a profit? If not, consider what other sources of income you have available until your business takes off.

Once you set a firm budget for the specified time period, research your product line, ensuring it fits within your budgetary means. Find out the profit margin on specific products you intend to sell. Determine how many you need to sell to break even and, eventually, to make a profit. You can make money selling almost anything online, but it is important to decide the amount of money you are comfortable investing before you begin your e-venture and to estimate how long it will take to recoup that investment and begin turning a profit.

Budgeting and accounting software, such as Quicken or Peachtree Pro, will help you keep track of money spent and give you control over the accuracy and thoroughness of the budgeting process. This type of software can provide assistance with allocating company finances based on your preset plan, forecast cash flow, and customer information and activity. There are numerous budgeting software packages, many of them for specific aspects of budgeting such as establishing trends. For example, Microsoft Forecaster can be used with a number of different general ledgers and works well with other Microsoft small business programs to automate the entire budgeting process. The Excel-based Exl-Plan Free generates fully integrated annual income statements, cash-flow statements, and balance sheets based on your projections.

Use the worksheet below to plan for necessary expenses before starting your business.

Expense	Amounts
Salary of Owner (if applicable)	
Mortgage/Property Taxes	
Advertising/Marketing	
Web Site Design	
Office Supplies	
Computer	
Computer Software	
Data Back-Up Service	
Printer/Fax/Scanner/Copier	
Digital Camera	
Video Camera	
Internet Connection	
Telephone	
Utilities	
Deposits for Public Utilities	
Taxes	
Insurance	
Interest	
Legal/Professional Fees	
Leases	
Inventory Purchases	
Office Equipment/Furniture	
Licenses and Permits	
Domain Name Registration	
Web Site Hosting	
Accounts Receivable	
Cash Reserve/Operating Capital	
Other One-Time Start-Up Costs	
Other	
TOTAL	

* Your total amount will depend on how many months of preparation you want to allow for before actually beginning operations.

Chapter 4

Business Plans, Licenses, and Taxes

Learn the Lingo	**Better Business Bureau (BBB):** A private, nonprofit organization whose mission is to promote and foster the highest ethical relationship between consumers and businesses. The organization keeps records on companies in good standing, as well as those with complaints lodged against them.
	Company philosophy: Usually the reasons why the company was formed, or an explanation of why it is in business or how it conducts business.
	Mission: The reason that a company exists. This is a company's purpose in the business world, and the main drive behind its goals and objectives.
	Industry trends: Ways companies may change the methods in which they conduct their business, deliver their products and/or services, or operate their organizations. It is often a new practice or way of doing business, driven by many factors, including profits, the economy, or customer demands.

In its most basic format, a business plan will typically spell out where you want your business to be within a certain period of time and how you plan on getting there. A well-written and organized plan not only assists a business through its birth, but is also necessary to get a business loan for inventory purchases or expansion. Over your business's lifespan, this plan will act as your road map. It can be changed whenever you see a need to update your business and expanded when it is time to grow. Many small businesses do not reach their ultimate goals because they did not spend enough time in the planning process. Creating a well thought–out business plan forces you to clearly develop and evaluate your strategic plans, and identify the opportunities and risks you are likely to face. By developing a business plan, you will better understand your industry, target audience and its needs, and the strengths and weaknesses of your business and competition.

Your plan will depend on whether you are working full- or part-time due to the differences in the resources you invest over time. If you are going to work part-time, it is just as important to develop this business plan. Managing time, setting priorities, and dividing resources necessitate precise planning. Writing a business plan may be one of the more complicated aspects of starting your online store, but there are many resources available for online and face-to-face assistance on a variety of business-related topics. The following are a few online resources available to small business owners. You may be able to make appointments with one of the representatives to personally discuss your needs.

America's Small Business Development Center Network (**www.asbdc-us. org**) represents member Small Business Development Centers in supporting small businesses throughout the United States. Its Web site provides informative articles, news, and links to useful resources and services for small business owners.

The National Small Business Association (**www.nsba.biz**) was founded in 1937 to serve as an advocate for small businesses in the United States. The organization now represents more than 150,000 small businesses.

SCORE (**www.score.org**) or Service Corps of Retired Executives is a non-profit organization consisting of more than 10,500 volunteers with more than 600 business skills. As a partner of the U.S. Small Business Administration, SCORE assists small business owners by offering resources such as advice and training.

The U.S. Small Business Administration (**www.sba.gov**) is an independent agency of the U.S. government that aids and protects the interests of small business in the United States.

It is often thought that strategic plans are only for large businesses, but in fact, it is for all businesses regardless of size. By creating a business plan, you are analyzing the strengths of your intended business to the opportunities that are available. In order to effectively accomplish this, you must research and analyze information about the business marketplace. It is also necessary to thoroughly understand the nature of your business, its strengths and weaknesses against the competition, and develop a clear mission, goals, and objectives. *See a sample business plan in the appendix of this book.*

Organization of a Business Plan

A business plan is broken up into many different sections, with each having an intended goal. From the executive summary at the beginning of the business plan to the financial statements toward the end, each section helps to build a thorough overview of your business as it is presently and as you expect it to expand in the future. A detailed business plan includes the following elements:

- Executive summary

- Mission statement

- Business structure

- Management team

- History and position to date

- Supporting documents

- Products and services

- Business strategy

- Financial plan

- Summary

- Industry overview/market analysis

The following sections offer a detailed look at the individual sections that will make up your business plan. You can find additional guidance online on these small business help Web sites:

- **http://articles.bplans.com/writing-a-business-plan**
  This entire Web site focuses on business plans and provides additional tools like business calculators to help you complete your planning.

- **www.homebiztools.com/planning.htm**
  This Web site also provides tips for creating your business plan and offers many other resources such as articles on business promotion and Web site design.

Executive summary

The executive summary will be the first thing potential investors see, so make this section stand out. It states the purpose of your business and offers potential financiers an overall view of the types of services or products you will be producing. The more detailed it is, the better — but try not to add anything irrelevant, like humorous anecdotes. The executive summary should be roughly a page in length.

Your executive summary should summarize the following questions:

- What is the purpose of your company?

- What is the current status of your company?

- What are the products or service you are offering?

- Who is your target market?

- What are your company objectives?

- What are your financial plans?

History and position to date

The history and position to date section asks for the step-by-step startup of your business. It should answer the following questions:

- What is the company's background?

- Why will your business succeed?

- If you have numbers through market research that indicate the need for your business, insert it in this section.

- Do you have any sales from previous years? If so, write them in this section.

- Does your company have any achievements or special publicity?

Your mission and vision statement

A mission statement is one short paragraph indicating the plan and purpose for your company. As you create your statement, consider aspects such as the ethical position, public image and branding, key strategic influence, target market, description of products or services, geographic domain, expectations of growth, and profitability. Your mission statement will be used for a number of purposes, including the incorporation documents. It should be included on your Web site.

Mission statements are simple to write and draw mostly on why your company exists, whom you plan to serve, and what your main goal is for the future. For example, here is a very specific mission statement for a fictitious candle-making business:

> "Comfy Candles, Inc. is committed to providing high-quality, naturally green candles for home décor and aroma."

Some companies also write a vision statement expressing future goals for the company. This is a short, precise, and motivational statement detailing what the organization expects to become and attain. The vision is often used as an inspiration for employees to set objectives and strategic goals. It describes future aspirations, without detailing how those will ultimately be achieved. A sample vision statement follows.

> "The goal of Comfy Candles is to be the leading online business of homemade, natural, and "green" candles. We will continue to provide our customers with the high-quality product they expect. Our commitment is to continually develop our products and services to enable our customers to meet their ever-changing interests."

Business structure

For this section, you need to answer the following questions:

- What is the business structure, and which state is it under?
- What is the reason you structured the business this way?

Selecting the appropriate business entity

When starting a business, you will need to decide what form of entity you want to establish. A business entity is a legal recognized form of business organization. The type of business you create determines what type of income tax return form you are required to file. A sole proprietorship, partnership, corporation, and LLC are the most common business entities. The following chart provides an explanation of the options available to you.

Legal Entity	Costs	Number of Owners	Paperwork	Tax Implications	Liability Issues
Sole Proprietorship	Local fees assessed for registering business; generally between $25 - $100	One	Local licenses and registrations; assumed name registration	Owner is responsible for all personal and business taxes	Owner is personally liable for all financial and legal transactions
Partnership	Local fees assessed for registering business; generally between $25 and $100	Two or more	Partnership agreement	Business income passes through to partners and is taxed at the individual level only	Partners are personally liable for all financial and legal transactions, including those of other partners
LLC (Limited Liability Corporation)	Filing fees for articles of incorporation; generally between $100 and $800, depending on the state	One or more	Articles of organization; operating agreement	Business income passes through to owners and is taxed at the individual level only	Owners are protected from liability; company carries all liability regarding financial and legal transactions
Corporation	Varies with each state; can range from $100 to $500	One or more; must designate directors and officers	Articles of incorporation to be filed with state; quarterly and annual report requirements; annual meeting reports	Corporation is taxed as a legal entity; income earned from business is taxed at individual level	Owners are protected from liability; company carries all liability regarding financial and legal transactions

For advice about your specific situation, contact a business consultant, accountant, or attorney. Additional information is available at **www.irs. gov/businesses.**

Management

When you are putting together the section on management and you are the only employee, you will only have to answer a few questions about yourself:

- What is your experience?

- What is your title?

- What are your skills and industry knowledge?

Products and services

This section will emphasize your current products and services, as well as your potential products and services. Any and all products and services should be listed here to show all potential investors what you will be concentrating on in your industry.

Industry overview/market analysis

This section includes an industry overview of the other major players or competition in the area and industry you are interested in. It does not matter if the majority of your business is online, at-home, or in a storefront; there will be competition. This section is where you summarize the competition and emphasize why you are different. The market analysis should accomplish these goals/answer these questions:

- Identify key competitors for each of your products and services.

- Determine your competitor's market share (what percentage of the sales they hold within the market).

- Is your business new or established? Will there be many more competitors coming into the field? Or is it stable at its present point?

- What are your competitions' strengths and weaknesses?

- How are your competitors satisfying customer needs?

- Are your competitors well-known, and do they have a strong following of customers?

- What are your competitor's weaknesses? What needs are they not satisfying for their customers?

- What barriers may keep you from starting a business in this market? For example, are any regulatory restrictions coming up that may affect your business?

For additional help with market analysis, *Entrepreneur Magazine* offers samples of analysis and planning forms for your business. They provide a variety of analysis forms, including competitive, demographics, market planning, cost analysis, location selections, and market research methods. *Entrepreneur* also gives advice with the following section on business strategy and financial planning.

Business strategy and implementation

Your business strategy and implementation section will focus on your business's approach, such as how you plan to execute your daily commerce, new products or services you plan to promote, and any marketing techniques that will be implemented to find clients.

Financial plan

In this section, you will have to answer questions about financial matters, such as your current annual net income and advertising budget. This section is a thorough breakdown of all the money coming and going out of the business, such as:

- Salaries
- Server cost
- Promotion
- Office supplies
- Insurance
- Inventory
- Maintenance
- Sales

Any other expenses you can think of, as well as startup expenses, will need to be added.

Summary

These are the last words your potential lender will read; make them memorable. This section should also provide a summary of your entire business plan in a concise manner. Be sure to sound confident about your business's future in this section.

Supporting documents

Any supporting documents you have, such as potential clients, financing reports, past client referrals, letters of recommendation, and/or any other supportive materials that might give a more in-depth overview of your company, should be submitted along with your business plan.

Business licensing

Licensing is by far the most confusing aspect of starting a business. Proper licensing is of the utmost importance — you could be fined, or have your business shut down. Familiarize yourself with the following business necessities:

Local business license

Most cities and counties require that you purchase a business license. The fees are based on different amounts, and it is best to check with your local business license office for details.

Vendor's license

Most states require a vendor's license when you collect sales tax. The taxes might be local, county, and state. Check the details on your state's Department of Taxation Web site. As an Internet business, you will be required to collect sales tax. For customers within your state, you must collect sales tax and pay it to the proper state agency at the end of the quarter. You will need this license to avoid paying sales tax on goods purchased for your business. A tax number will be given to you when you get your vendor's license.

Federal identification number/employer identification number (EIN)

All employers, partnerships, and corporations must have a federal identification number. Many sole proprietors use their social security number, but they can also acquire a federal identification number. The number is used to identify your business on all tax forms and licenses. You must fill out and submit file form #SS-4 to obtain your number. You can download the PDF form at **www.irs.gov/pub/irs-pdf/fss4.pdf** or request the IRS send it to you.

States are actively trying to convince Congress to pass legislation to tax all Internet sales. As of publication, businesses with a gross profit of less than $4 million per year are exempt from paying taxes on sales, but look for this to change. Err on the side of caution: Collect all required taxes and pay them to the proper federal and state agencies. Note what each jurisdiction requires, how often renewals are required, and the fee for each license or permit. Add these costs to your business budget.

Zoning

The purpose of zoning requirements is to monitor what activities are conducted in towns and cities. This helps keep similar businesses and residences in the same neighborhoods. Many small businesses, particularly service businesses, can be housed at home without violating local zoning laws, but check with your local jurisdiction to be certain of the requirements. You might be appropriately zoned for a home-based business, but you may not be allowed to put up signage, or invite clients or customers to your home. Retail and warehouse locations will require commercial or mixed-use zoning. Keep this in mind when researching licensing and selecting the location for your business.

Chapter 5

Your Business's Name and Location

When you go to the supermarket or a clothing store, you often look for a particular brand name. You are familiar with this brand because you have used it before or heard about it through word-of-mouth or the company's promotional efforts. You want your online customers to do the same. Visitors should come to your Web site because they have visited before and are returning, because another customer has recommended your site to them, or because they heard about your site due to your marketing efforts.

Branding involves establishing a visual voice and overall image of your Web site, aiming for visitors to identify with its concepts and remember your business over others. In their book, *Creating Powerful Brand*, Leslie de Chernatony and Malcolm McDonald define the word "brand" as:

> "...an identifiable product or service augmented in such a way that
> the buyer or user perceives relevant unique added values which match
> their needs most closely. Furthermore, its success results from being
> able to sustain these added values in the face of competition."

This definition focuses on what makes a brand successful: how a customer perceives a product as being better than the competition through personal relation to the brand. Branding in the "outside" world is as old as commerce itself. However, branding online is quite new, considering the first Web site was only announced in 1991. Amazon, Yahoo!, and eBay have spent the last decade successfully establishing their brand names. Yahoo! is definitely one of the most well-established brands on the Internet. The company not only offers many services in addition to its original directory, but it has built a large following of loyal customers by creating a distinctive, catchy brand.

Defining Your Business's "Brand" New Name

After you have settled on an online product niche and completed your business plan, you can finally begin to think about your business name and domain name. Do not try to reverse this process by choosing the name first; it does not work. Start thinking about your business name search by brainstorming ideas. Fill in the blanks of this sentence: My business, (*blank*), will target (*blank*) audience and differentiates itself from the competition by (*blank*).

This will clarify the message you want to convey about your business. Then, make a list of as many words as possible specifically relating to your business message, product, service, target audience, and characteristics. For help, look at the names of other sites selling similar products. Use your dictionary or thesaurus to look up synonyms, or ask your friends or family to help you brainstorm ideas. You can also develop a list of adjectives describing your business (for example, modern, professional, state-of-the-art, or expert) and consider using those in your business name. Which of these words are closest to how you perceive your business? Never forget how your niche makes your company different. If you provide travel information and services, you will want to include more specific words than "travel," "trip," "excursion," "destination," or "vacation" to provide customers with a better idea of your type of travel business. Instead, use more specific descriptions, such as "safari excursions," or "student getaways."

You will eventually find the best word or combination of two or three words to describe your business. For example, you may come up with "fashion shoe," "fashion shoes," and "fashion shoe store." These are specific words capturing your product and how it is different from other shoe stores. They are called "keywords" and are the words your potential customers will type into a search engine. Adding keywords to your domain name improves the click-through rate, or how often people click on your link to access your site. For example, the business's address **www.sanjoserealestate.com** encourages people who are searching for the keywords "San Jose" and "real estate" to click on this link.

The name of your business should clearly convey the products or services you sell. Consider a name that is short and concise but also catchy — something shoppers will remember and can spell easily. Names involving a play on words with a unique spelling are too difficult for customers to remember. Your Web site name should pertain to the target audience. For example, "Sick Shoes" means "impressive" or "cool" shoes for teens, but adults will not understand this lingo. However, if your products are directed toward teens or young adults, your name should reflect your customer base.

Creating Your Company Logo

Creating a logo is an important extension of your brand as it is the visual voice of your business. Your logo will be displayed on everything relating to your business, including your Web site, advertisements, business cards, coupons, letterhead, gift certificates, print and electronic newsletters, press releases, T-shirts, pens/pencils, free giveaways, and possibly even your car. Many times, people notice logos before any other aspect of a business's brand — including their Web site design and even their business name. In such cases, the logo represents your business. Think about the most famous logos in the United States. Do you need to see the name "McDonald's" to recognize the restaurant, or are the Golden Arches™ enough?

There are full books of theory regarding visual design, so unless you are familiar with how to design logos or are willing to put in the time to research the information, you may want to hire someone knowledgeable to help you design your logo. Because hiring an established professional could be a costly endeavor, you may want to contact the technical writing department at a nearby university and see if a student would like to help you. Many students are more than willing to take on a project like this just for the experience and for the addition to their portfolio, and because they are still in school, all of the theory is fresh in their minds.

If you insist on designing your logo, consider all of the design aspects and what meaning they convey to your customers. Show your logo to friends and family and ask for their honest impressions.

Typeface

If your logo has words in it, you need to consider how legible the typeface is, as well as what mood and voice it conveys. The typeface should reflect your business nature and appeal to your target audience. Say you are designing a logo for the previously mentioned "Comfy Candles" business, and want a professional feel so your middle-aged target audience is more likely to purchase candles from you. Which typeface looks more professional?

Comfy Candles   Comfy Candles

Notice how much harder the second example is to read. It has curly serifs (the little flourishes that extend from the ends of the letter strokes).

Some designers say that serif fonts are easier to read in print, while sans-serif fonts look better online. Others say the legibility depends on the design and that consistency in the font is more important. Here are some examples of serif and sans serif typefaces:

Serif fonts	Sans serif fonts
Garamond	**Futura**
Times New Roman	Helvetica
Cambria	**Calibri**
Bookman Old Style	Verdana

Color

If your business is going to operate solely in the virtual world, adding color does not cost extra. However, that does not mean you should go color-crazy. Think about how annoying those bright, distracting ads are that come with the morning paper, or that you see in cheap television commercials. You will also have some print items with your logo on them, so you need to make sure you can handle the costs of printing in color, or that the logo is equally as effective in black and white as it is in color.

Colors also have emotional and cultural associations. We associate certain colors as being "cool," like blues and greens, while others are "warm," like reds and yellows. If you have an exciting Web site meant to sell shoes to teenagers, you may want to include warm colors to indicate excitement. If you plan to target audiences in other countries with your Web site, you need to be careful with your color choices, because different cultures associate different meanings to color. For example, while Americans think of the color white as representing "purity" and "innocence," the Chinese wear white as a symbol of mourning at funerals.

Size

Many people think of logos as small, but what if you decide to add a large magnet to your car to advertise your new online business? Will your logo look as good blown-up as it does small? Do you have the capability of enlarging your logo without losing image quality?

Your logo can be created with a software program or by utilizing a graphic design professional. It can be an illustration or various visual elements, such as lines, curves, or shapes, which come together to create something interesting and abstract. If you are unsure of where to begin, look at your competitors' logos. Which ones do you like and why? Just be careful not to copy someone else's logo.

Choosing a Domain Name

Establishing a domain name is an important step to starting your e-business. A domain name is the Web site address people type in their browser to access your site, and it is the address that shows up on all of your promotional materials and in search engine listings. A typical domain name looks like this: **www.domainname.com**

Avoid using hyphens and numbers in your domain name, and be careful about using "my," "the," or a similar word in front of the name, such as "mybuttonshop.com" or "thedogbone.com," and plurals, such as "bluejeansstore.com." Customers often forget these words when looking you up online. If you need to do this, because the name you want is already taken, be sure to always use your business's full name in all your advertising. Do not say, for example, "Come to Dogbone for all your puppy's food," when the name of your store is "thedogbone.com." Similarly, if you cannot register a business domain name with ".com" and must use ".net" or ".org," always use the full name in all promotional efforts. For example, "Come to thedogbone.net for all your canine's chewables" uses your entire name and will let readers know where to find your business on the Web.

When you sign up for your domain name, you will find that many of the names you are considering have already been registered — or are very costly. Because so many people are selling online, millions of the .com names are already taken. You just need to be more creative.

Do not use generic names, such as Mary's Music Shop, Sam's Shoe Repair, or the Tire Retread Company. You will quickly be forgotten, if you even make an impression in the first place. Because these names are so generic, they are also hard to trademark. Names that have a specific location in them are not recommended, either, as people from all over the world will see your ads. Your name should not portray your business as being too wide or too narrow. The same holds true with the domain address. Consider how your business will grow in the future, and make sure the name of your business reflects this.

What about having a different suffix than ".com," such as ".org"? Domain services, such as **www.godaddy.com**, offer addresses with ".org," ".info", and ".biz" extensions. You may be tempted to buy one of these domains because the cost is less, or the name you want is not available in ".com". Although the other suffixes are becoming more common, people still associate .com with the Internet. Many users may not visit your Web site because they do not feel comfortable with the uncommon extension. These other extensions are also easier to forget because they are out-of-the-ordinary. Customers may try to visit your site using the .com extension, only to find another business or discover that the Internet cannot find the address. This will only frustrate customers. Yet you will find some marketers who feel using these uncommon extensions is a good idea because it differentiates you. Ultimately, it is your decision.

Domain Registration

Domain names must be purchased and registered. There are several reputable online sites, such as **www.godaddy.com**, offering this service. Go-

Daddy allows customers to register and maintain domain names for approximately $11 per year. If you purchase a hosting package, allowing your site to be maintained on GoDaddy's server, the price drops to $1.99 for the first year. IX Web Hosting (**www.ixwebhosting.com**) is another site used for researching and registering domain names. Through this company, you will receive three free domain name registrations when you purchase a hosting package supporting up to eight Web sites. This is a helpful tool if you want to create and oversee several different niche businesses at once. You can also get free domain name registration through **www.ibuilt.net**. Although the hosting packages are more expensive ($19.95 to $39.95 per month), there are a variety of features available. On each of these sites, you can find many name choices available for the yearly fee, for sale from the owner, or being auctioned off. If you already have a name in mind, and the registration company says it is taken, it may be for sale through the company that owns the name. However, check the Web site's history. You do not want to purchase a name through a site that once was shut down for spamming or other infringements.

Choosing a Web Site Host

A Web site host is a company that allows you to upload files to its server. These files make up the pages of your Web site. A server is a dedicated computer that can hold a large number of files, allowing visitors to access and view your Web site on an Internet browser. When choosing a Web site host for your site, things you should consider include:

Storage space for your files

Each text file, image, and design element of your Web site takes up virtual space on your Web site host's servers. The amount of space a hosting provider allows directly affects the number and size of the files you can use to make up your Web site. If you are building a more robust Web site that includes Flash animation or video files, those files will be stored on your hosting provider's servers as well, and will count toward your storage space allotment.

Hosting providers differ significantly in the amount of file storage space they will allow per account. Three hosting packages are available from GoDaddy.com providing 5MB, 100MB, or 200MB of storage space. A hosting package available from **www.hostmonster.com** offers 300MB of storage space.

File transfer allowance

File transfer refers to the process of uploading the files that comprise your Web site to a visitor's Internet browser. If a visitor accesses a Web page containing 20 photographs that are 2MB each, the file transfer size of those photographs is 40MB. If the visitor visits ten similar pages on your Web site, 400MB of your file transfer allowance are used.

Your hosting provider will give you a monthly file transfer allowance. Once you have reached your monthly file transfer limit, the hosting provider will either charge you for transfers exceeding your monthly allowance, or suspend access to your Web site until the allowance is renewed.

Exceeding file transfer limits may not be an important consideration when you first launch a Web site, but as your site grows in popularity, more people will visit your site on a regular basis. Choosing a provider that gives you a file transfer allowance of 1,000GB or more will help ensure you can keep the same hosting package for a year or more without upgrading.

Personalized e-mail addresses

This service allows you to send and receive e-mails from an e-mail address corresponding to your Web site. Customers would rather receive a response from yourname@yourwebsite.com than from a free account such as Gmail, Yahoo!, or Hotmail. Having an e-mail address that corresponds with your

Web site address looks more professional and adds to the customer's opinion that you are serious about meeting their needs.

Site design software

If you do not know Hypertext Markup Language (HTML) — the language in which most Web sites are written — or if you have never created a Web site before and do not want to spend a lot of time designing it, you can use Web site design software offered by some hosting providers.

The type of Web site design software provided by hosting companies allows you to choose from a collection of templates and then fill pre-set areas with text, images, links to other Web sites, and video files. The amount of control you have to customize the overall design of the templates varies by company and the software they use. Some software allows you to change the colors of the Web site, but not the layout; other software allows you to alter the colors and the layout. The more control you have over the look and feel, the more expensive the hosting package will be.

Look for a hosting provider that provides a demo of the design software. A video demo will give you a basic tutorial on using the software to create your site, but a limited free trial period allows you to try the software to see if it is simple to use and versatile. If a hosting provider does not offer a video demo or a free trial period, it is a good idea to look elsewhere.

E-Commerce Solutions

An e-commerce solution is a company that offers a wide range of services or specific software to help you start your e-commerce business. These services or software packages will allow you to design Web sites used for merchandising online products or services. They offer shortcuts into the e-commerce world, such as choosing from multiple predesigned Web site templates or using their virtual shopping carts on your Web site. There are scores of e-commerce solution providers, and many offer free trials or are quite inexpensive. You typically pay per month for the use of their services. You can use some of these companies for your Web site hosting needs, as well. For example, Volusion (**www.volusion.com**) provides domain names; merchant services, such as shopping carts and security safeguards; live chat installations; and marketing support. Volusion's packages run from $25 to $160 per month, depending on the services your business needs.

Make a list of the items you specifically want to utilize on your Web site, and find a provider offering those services. A virtual shopping cart, for example, would allow your customers to complete transactions for products or services via a Web site. With shopping cart software, you can safely accept and process different forms of payment, such as credit cards. First used by larger stores, such as Amazon and eBay, shopping carts are now standard for small businesses, as well. Compare prices and features among the many e-commerce solutions available. Many of these companies offer a free two-week or one-month trial period, or a 30-day, money-back guarantee if you are not happy with the results.

Getting feedback from other users is essential when deciding on an e-commerce solution because you want to your Web site to go live with as few glitches as possible. Join forums such as Small Business Forum (**www.smallbusinessbrief.com/forum/**) that give you the opportunity to communicate with other new Web site businesspeople, as well as the seasoned professionals who have valuable experience. Ask the e-commerce solution provider for the name of the last two or three companies that used its services, and find out if these Web site owners are pleased with the support they are receiving. Conduct an Internet search and read reviews about these companies' e-commerce solutions. Read reviews in magazines, such as *E-Commerce Guide* (**www.ecommerce-guide.com**) and *Internet Retailer* (**www.internetretailer.com**) in addition to "the best of" articles on blogs.

You can often find samples of Web sites utilizing the e-commerce solution's products on the company's Web site. Or, ask the company for a list of recent sites that have signed up for their services. Visit and browse these sites, and jot down what you like and do not like about the e-commerce capabilities. How well do the shopping carts interface with the Web site? Do the links work between pages? Do all the stores by this vendor look alike, or is there a way to customize the design template? After you have narrowed down your list of e-commerce solution providers to two or three, test out their customer service. Send them an e-mail with general questions, or call if a phone number is available. How quickly do they respond, if at all? How helpful were their customer service representatives? Is technical support staff available around the clock, and did they answer all your questions? To further help you narrow the field, visit the site's technical support area and see whether there is a video demo or a workbook to help you set up your Web site. How easy is it to use the template? Is this something you could do by yourself, or do you need to hire a professional Web designer?

What to look for in an e-commerce service

Because each business requires different services from their e-commerce solution providers, here are some features and characteristics normally desired by e-store owners.

- **Tool kit**: A variety of tools to get your new store up and running as quickly and as easily as possible in addition to features that maintain your site and provide you with ultimate selling potential. These include Web site design, shopping cart and payment options, reports, and marketing tools.

- **Simple setup:** A step-by-step guide on what to do and how to do it. If the service does not have technology that can give you all you need, it can recommend others who can. For example, if the e-commerce service does not have credit card processing, it can recommend other compatible services that are rated highly.

- **User friendly:** Once the site is running, it is easy to update and maintain.

- **Protection from fraud:** Merchants are given necessary tools to prevent fraud, such as requiring customers to provide the code on the back of their credit cards.

- **Help when you need it:** The service provider gives you the support you need from start to finish. Help may be available through phone, online chat, e-mail, blog, and/or a forum.

Partnering with Yahoo!, eBay, or Amazon

When you establish your business, you can also utilize the experience of an established e-commerce service, such as Yahoo!, eBay, or Amazon. Keep in mind, while these companies do offer outstanding service and exposure, you will still need to spend significant time on your marketing efforts. Some Web site businesses mistakenly believe that using a platform such as Amazon will automatically help to expand their business. It may provide more visibility, but cannot be used in lieu of your own marketing and brand-building efforts.

There are several different ways to build a business with Amazon. You can start small by signing up as an "Individual seller" (**www.amazon.com/ gp/seller/sell-your-stuff.html?ld=ASSOADPPricing**) and sell products without a Web site. If you expect 40 or fewer sales per month, you can sign up as an Individual seller for no monthly fee, but a per-product sale fee of $0.99. If you expect to make more than 40 sales per month, you can sign up for a Pro Merchant Subscription with a monthly subscription fee of $39.99, plus a range of selling fees (approximately 15 percent) on items that you sell. You can also go a step further and use Amazon as your Web site template. With Amazon WebStore, you sell your own products or services, but use Amazon's technology to create your site and utilize the e-commerce services you require, such as safe and convenient shopping carts. The template is easy to use, and you are given numerous widgets that offer different features you can add to your store, such as a "sale of the day," or downloadable music. You can sell directly from your WebStore or by listing products on Amazon. The monthly fee is $59.99 for as many Web sites as you want, and the referral fee is 7 percent. With Amazon, you can be confident that you are using a brand that is known and trusted worldwide. When customers visit your store, your Web site will utilize top promotional vehicles to encourage buying, such as discount prices, free shipping, or bonuses.

Yahoo! Merchant Solutions is another option for creating and operating their Web sites. Yahoo! requires a $50 setup fee. Then, you pay a monthly fee from $40 to $300, depending on the amount of sales you expect to make. You also have a sliding per-transaction fee of 1.5 percent to .75 percent, again depending on the number of your monthly transactions. When setting up your Yahoo! Web site, you can choose from a variety of designs. It is also easy to manage your online products. You can actually sell up to 50,000 products with your Yahoo! Merchant Solutions service. If you are only selling a few products, you can easily type them in to the online form to add them to your account. If you are selling hundreds or thousands of products, you will need to import each product from your Excel sheet to their online catalog. You can offer discounts and run promotions, as well as offer gift certificates for sale. Yahoo! lets you automatically calculate taxes and shipping and accept PayPal. The Yahoo! name is also well-established and will create credibility when associated with your Web site.

Which service is a better choice? You will find merchants who swear by either Amazon or Yahoo! because one of these opportunities better fits their needs. Some vendors feel they get lost in the myriad of products on Amazon. Others appreciate the fact that their product is competing against larger sellers. Some e-commerce sites think Amazon is too rough on its feedback policies and drops Web sites too quickly. Other Web site owners like the fact that their customers are judging them. Some vendors love the Yahoo! template's flexibility and say Yahoo! has many more design opportunities. Others say Amazon's layout is easier. The bottom line? Check both of these out very carefully, as well as other possibilities, such as eBay, if you want to go with an established company. Also, remember that there are millions of Web site owners who stay away from any of these structured platforms and go it on their own. They like the independence and ability to design and format their sites as they wish.

Whether you develop your own Web site, hire a design professional, use a company offering a Web site template, or affiliate yourself with a major e-commerce site such as Amazon depends on the type of products you intend to sell and the services you plan to offer to customers. Unfortunately, this book cannot give you a definitive answer on which avenue to choose. Each e-commerce Web site has its own priorities and needs. Once you determine your specific product or service, carefully review each of these structures and decide how your company fits into the parameters of these options. Then, study other Web sites selling similar products. Small business owners are usually eager to help other entrepreneurs, so, if possible, talk to the owners and find out how their sites were designed. What do you think of the Web site design — pros and cons? Is this site standing alone, or is it linked to a larger e-commerce business? What kind of marketing vehicles is the Web site using, either on its own or with a larger e-commerce site? Each option has its advantages and disadvantages. The platform you choose will not likely make or break your business's success — it instead depends on you and the efforts you put into your site. You are the driving force of your success.

Chapter 6

Creating an Effective Web Site

Learn the Lingo	**About Us**: For purposes of job hunting, the About Us section of a Web site is the introduction or a summarized version of the company, what it does, and what it is about. You can usually find it by clicking on a hyperlink on the top, side, or bottom of a Web page.

From day one, your Web site should be developed with the target customer's needs in mind and the desire to provide high-quality and effective service. From the moment someone visits your site, he or she should have a comfortable and positive feeling about your business. When building your business's brand, here are some important factors to keep in mind:

- **Your site needs its own look and feel.** Too many Web sites have cookie-cutter designs and are easily forgotten by visitors: People will click to the site and off again in a matter of seconds; nothing entices or encourages them to stay. There are many companies effectively using videos, forums, chat groups, and other marketing vehicles to achieve a unique customer attraction.

- **First impressions count most.** You must look credible and demonstrate to your visitors that you have the information, as well as the products and services they require.

- **Keep your word.** You must deliver promises made on your Web site. Do not advertise a big product sale is coming in two weeks and decide not to follow through. Earning your customers' trust is of the utmost importance.

- **Be what your customers want and more.** If your customers come to your site and expect "A" service and you give them "A+," you can bet they will come back.

- **Give customers a lot of information.** Whether you sell products or services, Internet users are looking for information in areas of personal interest. If they know your site always has something new, they will come back often.

Marketing

After you decide on your company name and find an e-commerce service, you are ready to begin the next stage of starting your business — marketing. Marketing includes almost everything you will do from now on that is not specifically related to your products or services, including designing your Web site and writing the site copy, to having contests in order to attract new customers. The marketing and promotional opportunities available to e-business owners like you are endless, and you are only limited by your time, resources, and amount of innovation. This chapter will cover some of these opportunities and how you can use specific tools and techniques to promote your business. Also included is a sample marketing plan to help you develop your own marketing and promotions program during your first year of business. Relatively speaking, planning the specifics of your business and preparing to launch your site requires fewer personal resources compared to what is needed to make sure people know your business exists, where it exists, and the reasons why it exists. It is not unusual for online business owners to spend an average of 10 to 12 hours a day on marketing-related activities. Other e-business owners work part-time and, while their income is commensurate with their time commitment, marketing is still an essential aspect for a successful business.

Marketing on the Web is different from traditional marketing and advertising. Online shoppers will never know you exist unless your business is ranked high on the search engine list. A large number of buyers will never go beyond the first page of Google listings to find a product or service, and it will take several months of daily marketing efforts to be listed high on the search engines. Marketing is a continuous necessity. In this and following chapters, you will be provided with a wealth of information on many different marketing possibilities, allowing you to find the avenue that best suits your business and your budget.

If you currently have a brick-and-mortar business and are now going online, you are likely to be ahead of the game when it comes to marketing. Tell your customers you are launching your online store as well. Add your Web site address on all your current print advertisements. Online marketing will be essential to the growth of your new Web site, whether you have a brick-and-mortar business or operate strictly online; otherwise, new customers will never know your business exists.

Creating an Attractive Web Site

The first step in devising your marketing plan is to design a Web site that will be pleasing and of interest to your present and potential customers. Internet users have become very sophisticated and expect sites to include specific design elements and user tools. Some design basics include:

- **Remember your target audience.** When you design your site, always keep your potential buyers and unique services in mind. A Web site selling high-priced vintage jewelry will have a very different design than a site selling elementary school backpacks.

- **Make it simple.** Today, it is possible to use widgets, audio, visuals, and Flash animation on your Web site — but it does not mean you should. Buyers want to find items easily and not be bombarded with a lot of extra "stuff." If they have trouble navigating your site, they will not stay, and certainly will not come back again. It may be helpful ask your customers for feedback on the site's layout. Some Web sites use many different fonts or typefaces in an attempt to display creativity and ingenuity. Rather than exciting readers, however, an overuse of font styles and sizes can be distracting. Choose a mixture of fonts correlating with your business's overall brand and style. More important than style, however, the typeface should be practical. The font used on your Web site should be legible and crisp to make for easy reading by customers.

- **Keep your colors to a minimum.** Stick with two or three complimentary colors at most. Avoid background colors that make copy difficult to read, such as a dark background with light-colored text. Use ample white space (also called negative space) to break up the objects on the page so it is easier to see the different areas of text and graphics.

- **Make links easy to find.** Customers will quickly become frustrated if they cannot find the link to their next destination. Use clear, descriptive text links, even if you already have visuals.

- **Remember, people view the top-left corner of your Web site first**. Put your important information there. However, if you have more than one page on your Web site, it will be impossible to know what page customers will see first, or where they will travel once they get to your site. Each page should include your logo and a navigation bar, making it easy for visitors to return to the home page. Also, each subsequent page should be as well-designed as the home page.

- **Include a sitemap in an easily accessible location.** Typically, these links are located at the bottom of each Web page. The sitemap gives the visitors a list of all pages that make up a Web site. For example, in addition to your products, you may have a blog, articles on your product line, and a live call-in service for product questions. You do not have the room to list these all on your home page. This sitemap "index" is another way to let your customers know of the features your Web site offers.

- **Give your customers easy directions on how they can get the information or products they want**. Using clear, linked headlines such as "Sign up here for our free newsletter," "Sale Items," "Place your order" are instant cues for customers.

- **Have an interesting mix of information and products on your home page**. Customers visiting your site are already interested in your niche and are always looking for additional up-to-date information, which can be provided through a general library of articles, a blog, or videos. The search engines will also pick up these articles and videos because they include pertinent keywords, hopefully helping your search engine rankings.

- **Make sure your Web sites load quickly**. Large images and other add-ons take longer to download. Customers may not have the patience to wait for the site to load and may jump to the next site offering similar products. Before you go "live," ensure your site loads appropriately on several different browsers, such as Firefox, Safari, and Microsoft® Internet Explorer.

- **Always display your company's full name, phone and fax number, address, and e-mail address in a notable location**. Some e-commerce sites only offer customers an e-mail address or, worse, an e-mail form. As online consumers become more leery of being scammed, they are starting to shy away from Web sites that do not provide specific contact information.

- **Consider hiring a professional Web or graphic designer to create a unique site**. Remember, however, that professional designers can be expensive and may not fit into the $1,000 budget set by this book. This may be something you want to consider once your business has begun to make a profit. To find a design company in your area, conduct a Google search or a find a freelance designer through sites such as **www.elance.com** to save money. Make sure you ask potential designers about other sites they have designed to see samples of their work. Graphic designers can also be used to create a logo or business signs.

Customer Connections Build Long-Term Relationships

Building a relationship with the customers entices them to visit your site for reasons beyond the products you sell. Customers who feel connected to your site for reasons such as the exceptional customer service you offer or the sense of community they feel with other shoppers on your forums will visit your site frequently. As you design your Web site, consider the following community-building features you can add to your site. You may not want to include all of these on your site, as an overabundance of features will make your customers claustrophobic. Yet, it is important to be familiar with all the features you can offer customers, and to keep them in mind for a later time to give customers additional tools.

Toot your own horn

Include an "About Us" section — an area on your Web site that not only tells customers about your background and how you got into the business, but lets them know why you are better than the competition and why they should shop with your business. Think about what part of your business makes you most proud. Do you have a unique business that no one else can duplicate? Even if your business is not uncommon, what do you offer that others do not? Maybe you provide an unusual product mix or the best prices. Perhaps your fashion background makes your homemade T-shirts the most distinctive on the market. Do you have a unique experience involving your niche that customers will be able to relate to? If so, emphasize these points throughout your Web site and in all marketing efforts.

Voice your own thoughts

Offer customers product reviews, a blog, and a newsletter or e-zine (an electronic magazine). These are ways you can offer additional information to your customers. If you are an expert in your niche, you have information that is valuable to your customers. Your customer should view you as a person who has considerable knowledge to share — not only on your primary subject, but related areas as well. You know your audience, and the topics that will interest them. If you are ever unsure of what your customers would like to learn more about, just ask them. Most people are not shy online. Offer feedback questionnaires to customers as a way to gauge their interest. Customers are likely to appreciate the fact that their opinions are important to you.

What do your visitors think?

It is just as important hear your customer's opinion as it is for them to hear yours. Offer customers a way to give you feedback and voice their opinions. Whether through forums, blog comments, feedback questionnaires, or product reviews, allowing customers to be heard goes a long way with customer satisfaction. This interaction with your visitors establishes closer relationships, helps you better understand their needs and interests, gives you a means for addressing suggestions and complaints, provides an avenue for feedback on your products and services, and assists in building a loyal community. Visitors always like to see input from other users, and it is also another way to attract the search engines to your site. There are a variety of ways you can receive input from your readers. Visitors like to voice their own opinions. Find different ways to encourage people to express themselves, or to let you know they have stopped by. You can ask for input on a specific product or topic of interest related to your niche. For example, if you sell homespun yarn, you can ask visitors about the types of items they knit. If you sell kitchen items, you can ask for suggestions on ways to buy pricey foods in more difficult economic times. A survey is another way of gaining feedback. Surveys can provide valuable insight into the demographics of your visitors. Offer a discount or free e-book to those who participate. Surveys can be used to gather name and e-mail addresses for e-zines and e-mails. Make sure to include an "opt in" section on your survey so that customers understand you will be sending them e-mails, to avoid hoards of annoyed customers and violations of the CAN-SPAM Act of 2003, which are the standards for sending commercial e-mail in the United States.

Feedback forms should be located in an easily accessible location on your Web site. Give customers the option to comment on the layout and design of your site, and the content and products you offer. Provide an e-mail address or feedback form to let visitors voice their comments, opinions, and suggestions. Feedback gives you a better indication of whether your products meet the customers' needs, or whether changes need to be made.

Be sure to include some of these positive personal comments in a testimonial section on your site. Your readers will want to know how others think, and they also are a testament to your credibility when new customers are browsing your site. The more your customers and visitors feel a part of your Web site, the more they feel encouraged to buy your products and tell others about you. Today, "others" can be thousands of people through forums, blogs, and social networking sites. If a business scams a customer, you can bet that the violation will be broadcast on Twitter, Facebook, or Google in a very short time. News travels fast, especially if it is negative. If your customers or clients are saying good things about you, let everyone know. Testimonials on your main page may initially feel a bit vain and cheesy, but within their own inner page, testimonials can be very helpful.

Provide the pertinent FAQs

A Frequently Asked Questions (FAQs) page can provide information to your visitors, build trust, and keep you from repeatedly answering the same questions. If a customer contacts you with a question, you can simply provide them a link to the FAQ page, saving you valuable time. The FAQs should, at minimum, help visitors learn more about your products and services and provide them with technical information on navigating your site. Topics FAQ pages can cover are: How do customers order products? What are your shipping options? What is the refund policy? How can they reach a technical professional for information on using your product? Depending on your products and services, your FAQ will have different questions and answers. When you write this section, put on your "customer hat," and predict the questions you will be asked most. Or, you may be writing this section because you have been inundated with customer questions. If so, include answers to questions you receive most from customers.

Give customers what they want

The options are endless regarding the features you can offer on your Web site. Your Web site should be a blend of unique features, like blogs and forums, and practical tools, like a secure virtual shopping cart and easily located contact information. Keep the material on your Web site fresh, and do not be afraid to specifically ask customers what they would like to see. After all, their opinion matters most.

Chapter 7

Generating Customer Traffic with the Written Word and SEO

Product alone, especially when prices among competitors are comparable, does not sell. You may conduct an aggressive advertising campaign, implement a multifaceted viral marketing program, and participate in several affiliate programs — but if your Web site does not have interesting copy, it will not generate adequate traffic. Content that advises, entertains, informs, and educates can attract and retain visitors and potential customers more than any other promotional tool. Regularly updating your site's content portrays you as a knowledgeable source about a topic of interest. Customers, clients, and potential buyers will want to come to your site if they know updated information will be available. In addition, you will get a great deal more visibility on search engines with informative and fresh news and articles because with this information, Web crawlers are more attracted to your site. This chapter will cover specific avenues for providing this information to customer. Articles, blogs, and e-zines will be discussed, as well as how to rank better among search engines.

Providing Content via Articles

Articles are a means of providing information to your customers. An article can provide a review of a new product on the market relating to your niche, or it can offer an opinion on current events relating to your niche. For example, if you are a photographer, articles relating to the history of photography, different types of cameras, photographic techniques, taking pictures of children, and photographing pets might be interesting topics to write about. For people who do not enjoy writing, this may sound like torture. You do not have to write scholarly articles. Use easy-to-understand language. People are not reading a novel, so the language should be concise and simple to understand. Writing at a sixth-grade level is generally acceptable, unless all your readers are well-versed in the subject and expect above-par writing. Write as few words as possible to convey your message, and avoid repetition. Ensure that your text is error-free; nothing turns off a potential customer or client like typos. Use your computer's spell- and grammar-check tools, and have at least one other person proofread your copy before posting it to your Web site. If you can afford the extra expense, hiring freelance writers to provide copy on a specific subject may be an alternative.

A word of caution: Do not plagiarize writing from another outlet. The content on your Web site should be completely your own. If you find an interesting article online, contact the author. They may be interested in granting you permission to republish the article on your site, as long as you credit the article to the author.

While writing your articles, integrate keywords into the title and copy to be picked up by the search engines. Keep a list of your top 100 keywords nearby while writing. Use as many keywords on your site as possible, including keywords in the titles, section heads, and product pages. By using keywords in critical areas of your site (on page titles and title tags, for example), search engines are more likely to rank your site higher. *Learn more about this in the search engine optimization section later in this chapter.*

Aim to publish a new article on a regular basis — at least weekly, if possible. After several months, you will be able to offer customers a library of articles. If other writers have granted you permission to publish their article on your site, include those as well. But do not provide a link to other outside articles on your site. The aim is to keep customers on your site as long as possible; sending them to another site to view an article is counterproductive to your marketing efforts.

Building Relationships with a Blog

Blogging is also a great way to communicate with your customers and get noticed by the search engines. Short for Web logs, blogs are a combination of online newsletter, forum, and journal, which revolve around a specific theme related to your Web site. Before publishing your first post, take the following steps to ensure you create the most effective blog.

Develop your theme

There are several approaches to blogging. Some bloggers write about whatever strikes them at the time. This type of blog is like a diary or journal. Others choose to write on a specific theme and continue this theme throughout the blog. Other bloggers have a general theme, but sometimes, if warranted, go in another direction. To develop loyal readers and build credibility, the second or third approach will be the most effective. Visitors with similar interests will return for new information. Look at the blogs of your competitors or others in your industry. What information do they include? How can you make your blog different to attract their readers?

When developing your blog's theme, consider the demographics of your customers. This should have already been determined when you formed your business plan. The topics of your blog posts must correlate with the interests of your visitors. For example, if you sell sunglasses to customers 16-35 years of age, write about sunglass designers, clothing fashions that relate to sunglasses, or sports that use sunglasses. If your products are targeted to an older demographic, write about how sunglasses impact the health of the eye, or new products designed for people with cataracts. You can write about product industry news you find in newspapers, business publications, or online. A Google search of "sunglasses blogs" locates blogs about sunglasses and new fashion, wholesale sunglasses, discount sunglasses, and tips on buying sunglasses. Remember your audience: Very few people buying sunglasses want to read academic articles on eyeglass design and development. Your blog should not only be informative; it should be fun as well.

Choose a blog service

There are several easy-to-use, free blog services, such as WordPress.com, Blogger, LiveJournal, Blog-City, and Xanga. Other bloggers use services charging a nominal fee. These companies often allow you to try the service free for 30 to 60 days. Many people use these blog software packages instead because they are more flexible and offer more design support. Typepad and Squarespace are examples of common blog software packages. Because everyone has different interests and technical abilities, the blog service you choose depends on your business's needs. Most blogs are simple to start. It is possible to create a blog within a half hour. Thus, if one blog seems too technical, simply try another. You will need to choose a title for your blog, which should mirror your product or service, URL, and Web site design. You can design the theme or look of your blog. Normally, several choices of color and layout will be available. It is important that these elements complement your Web site. If some design techniques are too complicated for you while creating your blog, such as adding photographs or links, just learn as you go. Most sites offer FAQ pages and technical support, or you can connect with other bloggers to get your questions answered.

Write your first blog post

Writing your first post may be the most difficult aspect of creating a blog, especially if you are better at math or technology than writing. Keep each blog post short — it should be just long enough to cover the subject, and include keywords to attract search engines. Looking at other blogs can help you create a style for your blog. You will find that blogs run the gamut on style, from short and to-the-point personal comments about a news item to 500-word articles that provide in-depth information. You will probably end up with entries of different lengths, depending on the subject and how it relates to your product or service. If you are writing about a topic you are extremely familiar with, pretend you are talking out loud. The first post should welcome everyone to your blog, explain why you started the blog, and give examples of topics you intend to write about.

When brainstorming ideas for your weekly posts, conduct an Internet search of your theme to see if up-to-date topics or news is available. Also, consider signing up for Google Alerts (**www.google.com/alerts**), which will send you a news alert each time your theme is mentioned in Google search results. This is an ideal way to stay up-to-date on your topic. Always elicit responses from your readers by asking them to send in articles. Readers can also submit photos of themselves if they somehow relate to your blog. Involving your customers in the blogging process will build community and lend credibility to both your blog and Web site. When someone does respond to your requests, remember to include a "thank you" on the blog page, or send the person an e-mail.

Keep on blogging

Patience and consistency is key with online marketing. Writing 20 blog articles on Monday will not throw you to the top of Google searches on Tuesday. Set aside time each day to write one or two blogs, and expect to see results within a few months. There are millions of blogs online, but a large number of these were started and never continued. Another large group of blogs never attracted the search engines and are sitting in some online limbo land. Unless you generate a blog post at least two times a week and continue to post until you begin to rank higher on search engines, your online marketing efforts will never pay off.

Get listed in a directory

After your blog begins to take off, consider listing it with a blog directory, which lists blogs by categories and offers a search mode for finding pertinent blogs. Doing so will encourage more people to visit your blog and lead to additional search engine listings. There are thousands of blog directories available, and new directories are created daily. You may not be able to register with some directories immediately. Many require you to write a certain number of posts before enrolling. Also, some directories are free, and others charge for their services. Research the directory before paying a fee. Some directories are very popular; others generate little traffic, have many categories with only a few listings, and have low ranking within search engines. After signing up with a directory, track whether traffic to your site has increased to determine whether enrolling in the directory is effective. The following is a list of some of the more popular blog directories.

- **Best of the Web Blogs (http://blogs.botw.org)**: This directory only accepts established blogs.

- **Technorati Blog Directory (http://technorati.com/blogs/directory):** This directory boasts tracking more than 100 million blogs on a regular basis.

- **Eaton Web (http://portal.eatonweb.com):** This is a paid directory, but it has a good reputation for its blog rating system.

- **Blog Search Engine (www.blogsearchengine.com):** This directory ranks high in the list of selective blog listings.

- **Bloggeries (www.bloggeries.com):** This directory is well-organized and easy to use. It also has a forum that will help generate traffic to your blog.

- **Bloggapedia (www.bloggapedia.com):** Spend some time looking at the categories of this community-based directory, and place your Web site blog in the right listing.

- **Blogcatalog (www.blogcatalog.com):** Do you want to know more about blogging while also promoting your site? If so, this directory is for you.

- **Blog Hub (www.bloghub.com):** This provides content from blogs all over the world, as well as lists separate blogs.

- **Blogarama (www.blogarama.com):** This directory has a large list of well-known and established blogs.

- **Blogtoplist (www.blogtoplist.com):** Users are required to place a button that links to Blogtoplist on their blog to be included in this directory.

E-zines encourage customer involvement

Electronic magazines, or e-zines, are simply company newsletters e-mailed to customers on a regular basis. They have the same information as blogs only in a different format; instead of posting a blog online, the information is being sent to customers via e-mail. The same information you include in your blog can also be sent via e-zine. E-zines are an excellent vehicle for marketing your small business. They can provide store news, ads, coupons, and new product information to customers. Customers should "opt in" or request additional information from your business before they are sent an e-zine. Because they have already requested additional information about your business, your e-zine subscribers are actually looking forward to receiving the newsletter.

The information in your e-zine can be posted online as well in order to allow for search engine recognition. Having both a blog and an e-zine allows for marketing toward two sets of groups — customers likely to read blogs and customers who generally only use the Internet to check their e-mail. The following are a few tips for creating and distributing your e-zine.

- Write the articles for the e-zine yourself. You are the expert, and customers want to see original information that cannot be found through other venues.

- Include articles about customers who have used your products. Let customers share their experiences and tips.

- Do not use your e-zine to sell products. Customers want information, not sales pitches. Instead, use a case study to explain how you helped a customer or client with a particular problem.

- Include product reviews or a "how to" about a product. Product reviews can be written by yourself or by customers.

- Use similar content in your blog and e-zine. While the same information can be included in both, add additional content to each so readers stay interested in both marketing vehicles.

- Ask e-zine readers to suggest other people who might like to receive your e-zine. Remember to get permission before sending e-zines to new customers through e-mail.

- Consider sidebar articles. For example, if your business sells grills, give your readers grilling recipes, or if you sell bat houses, write about the biology of bats.

- Have a question and answer section. Allow customers to submit their questions regarding your site or e-zine topic and answer their questions in your e-zine.

- Allow customers to write articles for the e-zine. Include a small note about accepting customer submissions. Remember to edit these for content and grammar before including them in your e-zine.

- Include a way for customers to provide feedback on your e-zine.

- Always remember to inform and get permission from a customer before including their name and information in your e-zine or blog.

Extra coverage for your e-zine articles

One way to build a list of individuals interested in your e-zine, and hopefully your Web site, is to write and place articles on e-zine submission Web sites, such as **www.ezinearticles.com** and **www.ezinearticlesubmission. net**. Google "e-zine submission" sites, and you will find a host of them. These online sites accept articles written by online writers, especially if the articles may be of interest to a large number of readers. When the e-zine is mailed to your customers, forward the articles to the submission sites as well. These sites will then send your articles to blogs and Web sites, and help you increase your search engine rankings. The following are a few reasons why you should use e-zine submission sites:

- They are a great source of advertising and offer excellent branding opportunities. At the end of your articles, you will include a "signature," or the name of your company and its Web site address. The site may also allow you to include a resource box or brief section with information about the author. They establish you as an expert and build credibility. It is easier to gain a prospective customer or client's trust when you are a published author. By engendering trust, you are encouraging people to buy your products or use your services.

- When articles are placed on submission sites, readers may be viewing them months after you first wrote the articles. Do not date the articles with information that will be out of date by the time the articles are read.

- Use the articles for other purposes. You should continuously think of ways to update and recycle your work. For example, you could conduct a Webinar or teleseminar on the article topic. Or, extend the article and publish an e-book.

Search Engine Optimization — Explained

While designing your Web site, you will read and hear a great deal about search engine optimization (SEO).

Learn the Lingo	**Search engine optimization (SEO)**: A marketing vehicle used to increase a Web site's rank among search engines.

Learn the Lingo

Directories: "Search indexes" directing people only to the sites they index. Directories are made up of businesses that have paid a fee to be listed. For example, if you want to have your store or business listed with a Yahoo! directory, simply pay the fee associated with the directory, and your registered business goes into a "categorized index," with other businesses having similar services or products. When a customer searches a directory using a keyword, the directory will only list those businesses that have paid for this service. The directory will not list matches throughout the Internet, as with search engines such as Google. When you list your store or business with both the search engines and the directories, you receive twice as much exposure.

SEO involves developing your Web site in a way that will give you maximum visibility with search engines. The more customers who see your products and information listed on Google, the greater the chance they will click on your business's link. Similarly, the closer your listing is to the top of the first page, the more clicks you will have. Understanding how SEO works is not difficult. Applying it to your site in a productive manner takes considerably more work. Web site marketing has become very sophisticated due to increasing advancements of the technology. With millions of Web sites competing for potential customers, it has become increasingly complex to ensure your Web site is found by interested buyers.

All Internet professionals have their own ideas on how to achieve high rankings. Search engines are often called "spiders" because they spread across the Internet, looking for morsels of information to bring back to eat. In this case, it eats words and phrases, and it prefers the newest, most interesting food it can find. These spiders, or search engines, hunt, retrieve, and collect information based on the keywords requested by users. They are searching for the most relevant results. Search engine spiders, therefore, study the content of Web sites and rank content by hunting for specific phrases. They use two or more related words or phrases to garner the basic meaning of your page. Providing relevant, frequently updated copy with the right keywords and phrases will attract these spiders.

Always keep in mind these two words: "fresh copy." Search engines seek out new content. If your content grows outdated, or you rarely add new copy, the search engines will overlook your Web site. Your Web site's home page alone is not enough to keep the search engines happy. Blogs or extra pages with additional copy attached to your main Web site are required to rouse the interest of a search engine. Most importantly, you need to integrate the keywords, or those special words pertaining to your unique product or service, into your Web site design, copy, and videos. Use a different title and description with keywords on each page. Remember: The title of the page is the most important SEO factor. Also, do not forget to include a sitemap on your Web site. The search engine spiders cannot index pages if they are not available. Sitemaps help search engines understand the layout of your site. Using these keywords will help you "optimize" your Web site and be listed on one of the first two search engine pages. Most users will not go further than this to find the product or service they desire.

Overuse of SEO keywords and other banned tactics

While using keywords on your site is necessary for SEO, overusing them can have a detrimental effect on your rankings. When Web sites are stuffed with keywords — so much so that the copy become unintelligible — search engines and customers know you are trying to scam the system. When this happens, the search engine spiders will stop visiting your site, and your site will eventually be ignored, resulting in low rankings.

The recommended keyword density ranges from 3 to 7 percent per article. Anything above this, even a 10 percent density, starts to look like keyword stuffing. It is even more important to have the correct density in the title, headings, and opening paragraphs. You can find keyword-density tools online to help determine whether your keywords are within the correct range. If not, find synonyms, or rewrite the copy.

Hidden text, another forbidden SEO method, occurs when the text and links are intentionally designed to be the same color as the background. Search engines will not only pass these over, but may punish you for such practices. This tactic is similar to hidden links or doorway pages, which are written into Web sites exclusively to achieve high rankings. Duplicate pages, with the same copy used repeatedly, are similarly nixed and no longer acceptable. The search engines are just as stringent on the number of links per page, monitoring the number of both outbound and inbound links. There are also programs designed to measure your link density.

Another SEO turnoff is using small or unreadable type to fit more words into the design of the Web site. The biggest "no no" in terms of keywords is one that not only disturbs the search engines, but your visitors as well. This involves adding keywords to your written text on your page that have nothing to do with the theme of the page. Today, keywords are important, but it is how they are used that matters.

Unfortunately, the SEO process is becoming increasingly complex because Google and the other search engines are continually changing their searching parameters. Because of this, many e-business owners use qualified SEO experts who are familiar with the latest changes. These professionals are hired to deliver SEO results by ensuring the Web sites are readily seen by potential customers. Also check with your Web site host, which may offer this service at an additional cost. Hiring a SEO expert can be costly, so you need to decide how much of your marketing budget will be spent on optimization. Consider taking on this responsibility yourself and putting aside a couple hours each day to ensure your Web site is getting the best placement. The more you are committed to the process, the better the results will be.

Chapter 8

Expanding Your Business Network

<table>
<tr><td rowspan="2">**Learn
the
Lingo**</td><td>**Internet profile**: A virtual portrait someone creates of themselves by answering questions and entering information. The profile can include photographs and other documents. A profile can be filled with personal and professional information, or a combination of both.</td></tr>
<tr><td>**Privacy policy**: The rules governing a Web site's use of information, which may be collected from someone who uses their site or who registers on their site.</td></tr>
</table>

The more exposure your business has on the Web and offline in the media and with potential customers, the more you will generate traffic to your site. Marketing should be one of your first priorities for expanding your site. This chapter will give you additional suggestions for building customer relations and publicizing your brand.

Developing a Marketing Plan

A major portion of your business plan should include where your marketing efforts will be concentrated. This marketing strategy should be clearly defined and regularly updated to ensure you are promoting your site in the best way possible. Here are some guidelines to follow:

Remember your niche. Consumers are becoming very knowledgeable with online advertising and are starting to pay attention to specific ads tailored to meet their exact needs. Forget broad marketing appeals that reach wide audiences, such as "Your baby will love our warm pajamas." Instead, develop a narrow message that reaches individual segments of your target audience, such as "You and your baby will love our warm and cuddly, organic cotton PJs."

Be consistent. Whether you decide to write a newsletter or blog, send it to customers the same day each week, month, or quarter. Customers will appreciate the regularity and look forward to receiving your mailings.

Try new marketing techniques. Once you are comfortable with the basics, devote part of your marketing budget to trying out new types of marketing techniques that are becoming vogue. In the online world, new marketing techniques are developed every day, and to keep up with today's tech-savvy customers, you need to stay abreast of changing technology. Branch out to pay-per-click advertising, Webinars, or podcasts. Develop marketing plans that integrate many different forms of advertising, public relations, social networking, and other forms of communication. They should all work together and enhance each other as a unified strategy.

Invest in yourself. Marketing a new business can be expensive, but it does not have to be. To learn about affordable marketing strategies, invest in "how-to" books, research ideas on the Internet, or attend a community college class.

Back to the Basics: Excellent Customer Service

You can develop an excellent marketing plan and employ all of the noted networking strategies, but if your product and customer service are under par, your business will fail. The customer does come first. With fierce online competition, providing superior service is a must. The following are just a few transaction issues that can cast a negative shadow on your business, resulting in a loss to your customer base.

- The item does not arrive, yet the customer is billed.

- The product is sent with flimsy or inadequate packaging and labeling, resulting in a damaged product.

- The item is received later than expected.

- The order is canceled without notice because it is out of stock or no longer available, although not listed as such.

- The customer has difficulty returning an item and getting a refund.

- The buyer cannot reach the business through e-mail, and no phone number is listed on the Web site.

- The condition of the item is not as described.

- The model number or brand is different than the one ordered.

- The item was not discounted as expected.

Joining Forums

Once you are sure that your customers are receiving the excellent service they deserve, you can branch out and begin to sell yourself to others across the Internet. One of the places to do so is in forums. There are thousands of different ones you can join, and you will want to join some forums to get additional information on how to expand your business and to develop relationships with peers. Also joint to meet potential customers, and use a search engine to look for forums corresponding to your niche. For example, if you are selling allergy-free candy to people who cannot have sugar, milk, or nut products, join forums on allergies, candy, diabetes, and parenting. Once you have found a few promising forums, find how many people regularly send messages, the quality of these messages (some forums are just another means for advertising and marketing), and how often people post messages. It is important to find a large, active community.

Before posting for the first time, spend a few days browsing the forum to get a feel for the users' styles and needs. Keep in mind forum manners: Be subtle, and do not blatantly push your product. Do not join a theme-related forum just for promotional purposes; you will be asked to leave when it becomes obvious. When you understand the forum's culture, respond to some of the comments by offering advice. For example, suppose you have joined a forum for moms with new babies. It would not be wise to push your product by adding a message such as, "Come to Baby Exchange and get the sale of a lifetime." Instead, answer a question a mom might have about how to compare natural cotton clothing to clothing made of synthetic material. Or, you could recommend forum members read a post on your blog relating to the benefits of buying organic baby clothing. On these forums, you have the ability to establish yourself as an expert in your field. Talk about your products from a learning standpoint, and try to remain general. If you offer practical advice and avoid appearing as if you are trying to make a sale, you will quickly earn the users' respect and curiosity. The members will recognize that you can provide valuable information both on the forum and at your site. Remember, at the end of each of your forum comments, you can have your "signature," which includes your name and business. Also, every time you print a question or response on a forum that is picked up by the search engines, you receive another extra link back to your site.

Customer Service via E-mail

E-mail offers an efficient way to provide feedback to customers. E-mail can be used to respond to product questions, clear up misunderstandings, relay order and shipping information, and encourage better relationships with customers. As you have seen from the previous section on e-zines, e-mail can also be used as a marketing vehicle to give the customers information on the latest products and the industry. Marketing e-mails are typically less lengthy than e-zines and usually only provide product updates and sale and promotion information. Customer e-mails provide customers a direct link to your business, giving them a means to provide feedback and e-business owners a way to improve customer satisfaction. The following are tips for effectively communicating with customers via e-mail.

- Respond to customer e-mails within 24 hours. This is especially important if the e-mail comes from a customer who just made a purchase. Answer any question regarding payment, order status, or shipment promptly. Consider setting up a separate e-mail specifically for questions regarding orders.

- Take several minutes at the beginning of your day to check all e-mail accounts and respond to customers. Even if you do not have a specific answer for the customer right away and need to research a problem, respond to the question. Customers would prefer an e-mail stating, "Thank you for your e-mail. I'll will get back to you within 48 hours," or "Could you please provide more information regarding your concern?" rather than responding days later — or not at all.

- To speed up the process of responding to common questions, simply copy and paste in a general response and add the customer's specific information to the e-mail. Also, if you have developed a FAQ page, answer the customer's question and provide the link to the page in case they have additional questions.

- After a sale, an automatic e-mail should be sent to the customer thanking them for the purchase and providing confirmation of the order, acceptance of payment, and notification of when the order will be shipped. Provide customers with a phone number or e-mail address in case they notice any problems with the order or have questions. It is customary to also send e-mail notification once the item has been shipped to the customer and provide them with the shipment tracking information.

- After the customer receives the purchase, send a follow-up e-mail asking whether the customer was satisfied with the product and the service you provided. If there were problems with the transaction, you want to know about them immediately. If you get positive feedback, ask the customer whether their feedback can be used as a testimonial. This is also a good time to ask the customer to opt-in for future marketing e-mails. In the e-mail, include a link to your opt-in notice on your Web site.

- Many companies offer customers a coupon or discount code once they have received feedback on the customer's recent buying experience.

- Use e-mail marketing sparingly. Customers will quickly become annoyed with businesses that send lengthy e-mails multiple times each day.

Social Networking Sells Your Business

The Internet is constantly changing, as are the ways it can be used to market your business. Social networking is the new "it" marketing vehicle. Many small businesses are finding social networking to be a great way to build and grow, especially in tough economic times when advertising budgets have been cut. Instead of paying for costly advertising, you are spreading information through word-of-mouth and Web sites that are generally free to use.

Although the exact definition is still being clarified, social networking essentially refers to an online community or group of users in which people can connect and communicate with others. Although the actual format may vary from one network to another, communication takes place in many ways, such as blogs, e-mail, instant messaging, forums, video, or chat rooms. Social networking connects people across the world in the privacy of their own home, and the networking sites are usually free and instantaneous. People can easily stay in touch with current friends, seek out old relationships, or establish new friendships. There are thousands of social networking sites, some that are primarily for social use and others that are also used for business networking.

Since social networking sites connect people who share similar interests, they offer businesses the opportunity to regularly communicate with customers, potential customers, and business partners who are interested in their products or services. Traditionally, networking consisted of business owners handing out their cards at monthly meetings or having a business lunch with a few acquaintances. The Internet has significantly expanded the reach of networking abilities. Instead of reaching out locally, businesses can use social networking to reach out to present and potential customers globally. A company's product line is still important, but it is closely linked to the relationships the business owners form.

MySpace was once the largest social network online; it helped spur a social-networking trend. Now, there are a number of other sites that have become more business-oriented, such as Twitter and Facebook. As a merchant, you need to impact a person's ideas and thoughts, and with social media, you can connect with a customer's interests. With social networking, businesses can add video, audio, and music to enhance visitors' experiences. Social networking sites also provide customers with a place to share comments, vote on polls, respond to surveys, or enter contests.

Social networking sites

The following sites offer businesses opportunities to network with other business owners.

- Bizfriendz (**www.bizfriendz.com**): Make new contacts, promote your products and services, get viral exposure to your business, and earn commissions while you build your network.

- Biznik (**www.biznik.com**): Their tagline: "Business networking that doesn't suck." Geared directly to entrepreneurs and business owners, with a number of different communities.

- Cofoundr (**www.cofoundr.com**): A private community for entrepreneurs. Promises to help members build teams and network with other entrepreneurs.

- Digg (**www.digg.com**): Locate articles online about your business, yourself, or something of interest to potential customers, then post them on the site. You can also find articles of interest others have put up on the site for readers to rate.

- Ecademy (**www.ecademy.com**): Provides extra tools to build your business, such as networking events, Webinars on online topics, and the ability to locate members with specific knowledge.

- Fast Pitch (**www.fastpitchnetworking.com**): Reports it is growing faster than any other social network for professionals. Set up your own profile page and network with other businesspeople.

- Konnects (**www.konnects.com**): Gives each member a profile page. Join communities, meet other members, and network with professionals with similar interests.

- LinkedIn (**www.linkedin.com**): Connect and network with others in your field or those who can use your abilities and/or services.

- StartupNation (**www.startupnation.com**): Active forums with a wide variety of subjects for businesses.

- Stumble Upon (**www.stumbleupon.com**): Post any information of value and interest to others.

- Upspring (**www.upspring.com**): Increase exposure and attract more customers. Sign up for free and get a profile page, find and join groups, and increase your networking activities.

- Xing (**www.xing.com**): An active group of professionals looking for ways to network with people of interest.

In addition, you will want to spread the word through more personal networking sites. These include:

- Facebook (**www.facebook.com**): Connects people with friends and others who work, study, and live around them.

- MySpace (**www.myspace.com**): Find friends and classmates, meet new people, listen to free music, share photos, and watch videos.

- Twitter (**www.twitter.com**): Share short thoughts with others about what is immediately happening.

- Flixter (**www.flixter.com**): Share movie reviews and ratings with friends.

- Tagged (**www.tagged.com**) Allows users to send messages, leave comments, browse photos, watch videos, play games, give tags, and chat.

- Classmates (**www.classmates.com**): Connects 50 million members locate friends and high school alumni to share memories, class reunion information, and yearbook pictures.

- LiveJournal (**www.livejournal.com**): A site for journaling and blogging with privacy controls, photo storage, publishing tools, and style templates.

Offline Networking

Regardless of how you are marketing online, offline, face-to-face networking within your community remains a powerful marketing tool. Do you belong to local networking groups? Many communities form small networking groups made up of a variety of different businesses. The purpose is to network, and to share leads and information. Also, you should join your local chamber of commerce, downtown association, newcomer's group, or other business-networking group that usually sets aside time for the members to mingle and discuss their business products. Chamber of commerce meetings are often conducted by their members, which will give you an opportunity to focus on your business. Additional networking time follows the meeting to allow business owners time to mingle and discuss their business and products.

Participating in industry-related associations can also be helpful for building your business.

Attend a few meetings to determine whether the group fits your goals. If so, become a member and volunteer to fill an active role. Some Internet-specific groups include:

- Society of Internet Professionals (**www.sipgroup.org**): Consists of individual Internet professionals and companies, as well as educational institutions, and provides a forum for members to help build the future of the Internet.

- U.S. Internet Industry Association (**www.usiia.org**): A trade organization for online commerce, content, and connectivity. It offers education on Internet-related and technology issues, advocates Internet public policy, and provides business news, information, and support services.

- Association of Web Professionals (**http://webprofessionals.org**): Strives to improve the credibility of Web professionals through professional development availability, such as its certified Web manager examination, standards, and code of ethics.

- Computer & Communications Industry Association (**www.ccia-net.org**): An international nonprofit organization consisting of senior executives representing all sizes of computer and communications firms. Its mission is to advance the members' businesses by supporting open, barrier-free competition in computer and communications products and services throughout the world.

Become involved with your local community. Consider volunteering locally to network with others in your community. Wear your logoed clothing, such as a T-shirt or jacket, whenever you volunteer at the soup kitchen, meet with members of your church or synagogue, or volunteer at your child's school. Donate your products and services during the holiday season and for special events throughout the year, especially when there is an emergency or celebration. Organizations holding fundraising events are always looking for local businesses to offer donations or to sponsor an event for their cause. You products or services can be used as door prizes or can be raffled off. These ideas not only offer solid advertising opportunities, but also help to build your business's reputation within the community.

Successfully Using Public Relations

Public relations is the "free" aspect of the marketing plan. This is a non-advertising, unpaid way to get your name out to potential customers. The response you receive from public relations is not as automatic as an advertisement for a major sale, but over the course of your efforts, it can impact your reputation — hopefully positively, but sometimes negatively. Public relations includes free articles in newspapers, giving a luncheon speech to a local chamber of commerce, setting up a booth a local health fair, and talking to school children.

For example, when you first launch your Web business, you should contact all the local media so they can run an article about your new venture. Later, you will continue to garner publicity by keeping your local media informed of newsworthy events in which you are involved. Establish a relationship with a local reporter, and submit relevant and timely press releases. Also, remain in the public eye by volunteering for local organizations and in community events. Publicity can also be leveraged online. By distributing press releases to various online media outlets and press release distribution Web sites, such as PR Wire (**www.prwire.com**) and PR Web (**www.prweb.com**), news about you and your business may be featured in an online forum, article, or story, drawing potential customers to your site.

The invaluable list of names

Everything you do to market your name will help you make contact with potential customers. It is typical practice to employ advertising, promotions, free giveaways, and contests to develop a list of customers who can be contacted for future marketing purposes. When opting-in to receive e-mails from your business, customers are providing personal information that must be held private. Most businesses have privacy statements on their Web sites specifying how personal information will be handled. There usually is a link at the bottom of the Web site that says "Privacy Policy." Visit other Web sites to see how this policy is typically worded. Send customers only what they have agreed to receive.

Customers should be given the chance to opt-in to receive information from you at all possible times. Offer virtual comment cards on your Web site, and include a space for customers to provide their e-mail address and mark a box indicating they would like to receive promotional material from your business. Once you begin sending promotional material to the customer's inbox, customers should always be given the chance to unsubscribe to your e-mails if they have changed their minds. Following these practices will protect your company from violating the CAN-SPAM Act of 2003, which regulates e-mail solicitations nationally. No matter what type of business you decide to start — whether it is one of the suggestions in the following section or another similar one — always keep marketing in the forefront of your mind. This is the way you will make your Web site stand out from the myriad of competitors.

The next section of the book offers 199 Internet-based businesses you can successfully start for less than $1,000. As previously mentioned in the introduction, you will find a general business area with examples and then sideline businesses, or niche spinoffs, to show you how these businesses can be customized based on your expertise. There are even some examples of the newest and most unique niches. Have fun.

Section II:

199 Internet-Based Businesses

Chapter 9

Advertising

#001 Advertising Network Service

Business overview

Do you have an interest or, better yet, experience in online advertising? Are you comfortable with extensive online research? Couple Internet experience with skills in advertising and sales, and this may be the right business for you. As an advertising network specialist, you can help businesses get the visibility they need within the online community. Internet advertising has become so sophisticated and complex that specialists are needed to ensure businesses are spending advertising dollars wisely and to help generate additional revenue by hosting ads on their sites. Advertising networks connect Web publishers hosting advertisements with business owners who are interested in running ads. As an advertising network specialist, you will work with businesses to find appropriate means of advertising that fit their needs. You will first meet with your clients to determine these needs and research different advertising leads — whether it is through banner advertising, text links, pop-up ads, or e-mails — and present your findings to your clients. After you find advertising vehicles meeting their requirements, you will assist your clients with connecting with these leads.

Skills needed

An understanding of effective advertising. The ability to create online advertisements.

Tips

Establish strong relationships and trust with your customers. This can be more important than the product itself. Always offer a good product at a competitive price.

Where to find more information

The Network Advertising Initiative (**www.networkadvertising.org**) is made up of online marketing and analytics organizations committed to consumer awareness, and responsible business and data management standards.

#002 | Coupon Business

Business overview

People are always looking for ways to save money on items they purchase regularly. According to comScore (**www.comscore.com**), a company that monitors Internet commerce and trends, in 2008, Web sites offering coupons saw a 38 percent increase in total page views. Due to current economic conditions, coupon clipping is once again becoming popular among consumers. Consumers are looking for even small discounts on all products, including groceries, oil changes, clothing, and vacations. With online coupon Web sites, consumers can download and print coupons or access discount codes for purchases made online. Due to the growing demand for discounts and the need to attract new customers, retailers look for new avenues to distribute coupons or special discounts. Retailers are hoping that by offering consumers coupons, they will try their product or service for the first time and become repeat customers, or spend more money than they would have without a coupon. With online coupons, merchants create coupons, each with a unique serial number, which are printed by customers and redeemed in stores, or merchants offer discount codes for purchases made online. Coupon Web sites offer retailers the opportunity to distribute their coupons to new customers. Your coupon Web site will charge businesses for placing coupons on your site, and in some cases, you may get a commission from the business when a coupon is used. Another option for this business is to make additional income by charging advertisers to appear on your site. Many Web sites offering services such as this make an income in this manner. Advertisers will pay big bucks to advertise on a site that attracts a large number of customers. Market to advertisers that relate to the area of business you are covering. In this business, SEO is very important to get people to your site. Also, most coupons come with expiration dates, and it is important to make sure all your coupons are always up-to-date.

Skills needed

Good Web searching abilities.

Tips

To keep advertisement costs low, find other ways to get people to your Web site, such as developing a mailing list, networking with as many other sites as possible, and getting the word out through press releases and articles.

A coupon site must have an attractive design, the latest savings, a well-organized layout, and coupons that are easy to download and print.

One bad coupon can spoil the site and your reputation. Make sure that all coupons are timely, and that the product is available by checking the coupons on your site regularly.

Where to find more information

Entrepreneur Magazine (**www.entrepreneur.com/businessideas/518. html**) "How to Start an Online Coupon Business."

Retail Me Not (**www.retailmenot.com**) offers printable coupons as well as codes for many well-known businesses, such as Papa John's and Victoria's Secret.

The Penny Pincher Gazette (**www.ppgazette.com**) offers printable grocery coupons and recipes that use the discounted ingredients.

#003 Banner Advertising Artist

Business overview

Banner advertisements appear all over the Internet as small rectangular ads. Advertisers hope the visitors to a particular site will click on the ad, visit their Web site, and buy their product. If that "click-through" does not take place, advertisers want consumers to remember them in the future and visit the site at another time. As with all advertising, the product or service must be of interest to the consumer; however, the design of the ad should help motivate consumers to click on it. As with traditional advertising, there are scores of artists who can design ads. Web site merchants are looking for a design that will entice potential customers to click on the banner and buy the product. The designer must understand the advertiser's business and the target market. As a banner designer, you will work closely with the advertiser to ensure you meet their specific requirements. You need to creatively design a banner with the right look and feel for client's needs. It may be necessary to develop a series of different design concepts to present to the client. You will either be paid by the job or per hour, and may be asked to be available to do a certain amount of work each month.

Skills needed

Fluency in graphic design and the software involved with this industry, including HTML, Flash, and other similar software assignments A true understanding of advertising. Previous experience in the field and, possibly, a degree in graphic design.

Tips

To attract your first customers, offer specials, such as "Two designs for the price of one or the first design is free." Consider working only in certain niche areas to become recognized for your unique style.

Where to find more information

Design Firms (**www.designfirms.org**) is a directory and social networking site for Web designers, developers, and graphic designers.

#004 Internet Keyword Advertising Specialist

Business overview

A keyword advertising specialist helps e-commerce business owners determine the most effective terms and phrases to include on their Web site to attract search engines to the site — thus increasing customer traffic. Because search engines are continually changing search parameters, it often takes an online professional to determine the most effective advertising keywords to use. An increasing number of small businesses are relying on Internet advertising to promote their products to potential buyers. Advertising online is one of the most economical ways to sell goods or services. To increase the number of leads obtained from online advertising campaigns, e-commerce businesses must know which keywords are the most effective at generating traffic to their site. Online advertising is becoming so sophisticated that it is possible to track leads per advertising keyword, cost per lead, and dollar cost per sale. Businesses are able to select keywords for their online advertising campaign and track the effectiveness of each of these words in relationship to sales and revenues. This is the indeed the power that Internet advertising provides. However, not all e-commerce owners have the ability to determine which keywords are the most effective, and many are not familiar with new technological advances in Internet advertising, such as SEO and analytics. As a keyword specialist, you will advise e-commerce businesses about using the techniques that will be most effective for their advertising campaigns. You will help businesses determine the correct keywords for their niche, where to include keywords on their Web site, and how to regularly update the site with fresh information to attract search engines.

Skills needed

An understanding of how search engines work.

Tips

To find new clients, contact businesses that have brick-and-mortar stores and are advertising online for the first time.

Where to find more information

Majon International (**www.majon.com**) offers a slew of advertising services, one of which is keyword advertising.

Sideline Businesses

#005 "Opt-In" E-mail Marketing

E-mail marketing consists of working with businesses to develop mailing lists of potential customers who might be interested in receiving more information from a business. The only ethical way businesses can get a potential buyer's e-mail address is by its owner explicitly giving permission or "opting in" to receive these e-mail advertisements. Opt-in or personalized e-mail marketing qualifies prospects and makes them more open to advertising offers. In this capacity, you help your client devise ways to reach targeted audiences and encourage them to subscribe for more information through e-mails.

#006 Press Release Distribution

This publicity mailing through both print and online media can greatly increase a business' sales, expose a company to the large population demographics, and considerably enhance the image of an e-commerce products and services. In this business, you will assist businesses with finding appropriate venues for press release distribution — both off- and online — and with writing and distributing the press releases through these venues.

#007 Fax Advertising

In this business, you will assist clients with developing a list of fax numbers for potential customers for distributing advertisements. This method of advertisement delivers a specific message in a very effective and focused manner. This is similar to e-mail advertising in that businesses sometimes must opt-in to receive these advertisements. You should ensure businesses have opted-in to avoid violations of the CAN-SPAM Act.

#008   Magnetic Car Signs

Business overview

People are always coming up with new ways to market their businesses. Recently, marketing has spread from billboards and newspapers to automobiles. Magnetic signs on cars advertise the company and display a tag line — just enough to interest the buyer. These signs are vacuum-formed, three-dimensional plastic sheets with magnets on the back to attach to the car. Many people see this form of mobile advertising as customers or employees drive around town. As with any other business, magnetic sign entrepreneurs are always coming up with a new look, such as metallic or relief lettering. To start a complete business, you should plan to design and manufacture the sign. Check into used equipment to lower your overall costs. You will need a software package to design the layout. The signs are made by heating a 28- x 16-inch white vinyl plastic sheet in a vacuum machine until it becomes soft, then using a vacuum pump to place it over an arrangement of letters. When the vacuum process is complete, the impression of the letters is on the sign. The sign is then trimmed, the magnetic strip applied, and the lettering painted with rollers and ink. You can purchase a wide variety of lettering, borders, and arrows, but adding a company's logo to the sign may require more work. Unless you are already familiar with making these signs, you should find someone in the business who will show you the ropes. It takes time to learn in the ins and outs, and you lose money each time you make a mistake. Also, there are a couple of different ways to make these signs, each with pros, cons, and ways to save money.

Skills needed

This business requires intricate and painstaking work, so patience is a must.

Tips

Form joint ventures with advertising companies that want to offer this service but do not have the capability.

When you are designing the layout, check and recheck the spelling of the company name. Today, many names are lowercase letters or two names combined. Do not guess at the spelling of other words. When the design is ready, have the customer approve the final product.

Where to find more information

The International Sign Association (**www.signs.org**) is a trade organization made up of manufacturers, suppliers, and users of visual communications including signs.

Sideline Businesses

#009   Automobile Bumper Stickers and Decals

People love to express their opinions and interests via bumper stickers. The software to make these is low-cost and easy to use. In this business, you can make generic stickers or customer stickers for businesses or single customers. Either way, design several different kinds and show them off on your Web site. The wittier they are, the better chance you have of making sales. For more information on using a printer to print your stickers, do an online search for printers, such as **www.ripped-sheets.com/inkjetlaserblankprintablebumperstickers.html**.

Sideline Businesses

#010   Small Advertising Signs

In order to attract more attention to their stores, many small businesses are now using wire stake signs. These signs are also used to promote political candidates, advertise contractors, and point out new homes for sale. Businesses, political parties, and real estate agents know that small advertising signs with frames and stakes provide a practical marketing method that works. With one quick glance, a prospective customer gets all the information needed to take the next step. With creativity, you can make attractive and colorful custom signs that are all shapes and sizes, and that build a positive image for your customers. You can make your own design with Microsoft, Photoshop, or Adobe software applications, have the message printed, apply it to the plastic, and put it in the wire frame. To advertise, include your business's name and phone number on the signs, and place them in high-traffic areas. Give some of your signs away for free to real estate agents or contractors who have a large number of properties. Word-of-mouth advertising is very helpful in this line of business. Every town has different regulations for where signs can be placed. Check with your town hall.

Chapter 10
Animals

#011 Pet Sitting

Business overview

People love their pets, but they often are not home to enjoy them as much as they would like. They work during the day, are on trips for pleasure, or spend a lot of their time running many different errands. A reliable person to take play with and care for their pets is always in demand. If you feel comfortable with all types of animals, including dogs, cats, birds, fish, and even snakes, this may be the job for you. Pet sitters exercise, feed, and groom animals and sometimes give medication or injections. You may also be asked to water plants, take in the mail, and clean an animal's living area. The client may ask you to stay at the house for an extended period of time, or come in a couple of times a day to take care of an animal. It goes without saying that you need to love animals of all sorts — even reptiles and rodents. Each animal has its own temperament and special type of care, and you should be familiar with how to care for an animal before agreeing to care for it. You may want to consider taking a few courses in dog training and emergency medical care. Create a contract including specific services you will provide and the payment requested. It will be necessary to find enough pet-sitting jobs to support your needed income. Word-of-mouth marketing, both off- and online, will promote your services. Make sure you come up with a clever name that people will remember easily, and design cards and fliers to put in pet shops, veterinarian offices, and related stores. Send a press release and photo to local media announcing your new business, and advertise your Web site with newspapers or coupon magazines. Use SEO to increase your rankings among search engines. You will want to be sure you are listed high geographically and within the locations where your customers live. Social networking with others in your geographical area will also be helpful. Put together a list of solid references and phone numbers, and look into sending a direct mailing to these potential clients. Check into liability insurance to protect yourself should an accident occur while watching a pet.

Skills needed

It goes without saying that you need to love pets of all kinds. Each animal has its own temperament and special type of care, and you must be familiar with its needs and behavior. Take courses in dog training and emergency medical care, and read instructional books related to the animals.

If you are doing this as a Web business, make sure you know your online marketing inside and out.

Tips

Ask the owners what you should know about their pet to avoid surprises when they leave. Spend some time with the animal while they are still at home.

If you will be traveling a considerable distance to a house once or twice a day, include your time and travel expenses in your fees. These costs can add up quickly.

Another option for this business is to make additional income by charging advertisers to appear on your site. Many Web sites offering services such as this make an income in this manner. Advertisers will pay big bucks to advertise on a site that attracts a large number of customers. Market to advertisers that relate to the area of business you are covering.

Where to find more information

Pet Sitters International (**www.petsit.com**) is a membership-based advocacy group with more than 8,000 members worldwide.

Sideline Businesses

#012 Dog Walking Service

A dog walking service is perfect for people who love animals and do not want a nine-to-five job. Depending on the owners' schedule, you will walk the dog once or twice a day. You may want to talk with an animal trainer to learn the proper way to walk different types of dogs. Do not accept an assignment if you feel uncomfortable with the dog's strength or unfriendly behavior. Create a contract describing the services you will provide and the expected fee. Check into liability insurance. Your town or state may require you to have a license. Rates will depend on where you live, so find out what your competition is charging. Design a Web site to advertise your services and to develop an online marketing plan, letting people in the area know your services are available. Visit The Doggie Walkers (**www.doggiewalkers. com**) for more information.

Sideline Businesses

#013 Pet Sitting Matching Service

Another option associated with pet sitting is to start a Web site that matches pet owners with pet sitters. You can match these services for people around the country and charge the pet sitters a fee when a successful match has been made. You can also allow other businesses to advertise on your Web site to bring in additional income. Visit **www.pet-sitters.biz** for an example of a successful pet sitting matching service.

#014 Pet Portraits

Business overview

People often see their pets as part of the family and want to hang their picture on the wall. If you are artistic and know how to use computer applications such as Adobe Photoshop or Corel Paint Shop Pro, you can expertly transform a photograph into an artistic portrait that owners would love as a special addition to their home décor. Of course, you can also take photos of pets through traditional means without the use of design software. Your pet portrait can also be perfect for birthday, housewarming, anniversary, or Mother's or Father's Day gifts. In 2008, approximately $43 billion was spent on pets in the United States — more than the gross domestic product of all but 64 countries worldwide. You can use your artistic and computer design skills in a variety of ways to make memorable pet portraits. Online businesses already offering this service vary considerably, including black-and-white sketches, watercolors, and oil paintings. The design techniques differ based on the artist's level of computer skills and fine art experience. Many Web sites offer the standard photo-to-art program that comes with the software package and requires little design experience. However, some artists actually use the software applications to completely recreate the photograph stroke by stroke, adding detailed layers with sketching, high-lighting, and coloring. Other artists eliminate distracting items or alter the photograph's setting, such as changing the background from a living room to an outside location. Some designers totally delete the background and produce a colorful backdrop. Clients can choose to have the photo printed on canvas or fine art paper. Your charge will be based on the size of the final artwork and the amount of time you spend on a project. You can charge extra for special effects, cropping, or retouching. With the right software package and your artistic creativity, you can transform a customer's digital photo into an heirloom painting.

Skills needed

You need a thorough understanding of computer design, as well as the artistic ability to utilize the software and enhance the photographs using your creativity.

Tips

On your Web site, offer a blog providing additional tips and ways that customers can change the look of their pet photos.

Because the portrait software is relatively easy to use, many businesses offer a satisfactory but low-end painting with little or no design. To be competitive, you must differentiate yourself from these low-cost services by finding a unique angle and offering a high-quality product that shows off your artistic abilities.

Where to find more information

The Association for Pet Photographers (**http://bppa.ws/pet-animal-photography**) is a member-based site listing pet photographers from around the world.

CASE STUDY: CAROL LEW

Carol Lew
Old World Pet Portraits
452 Washington Mountain Road
Washington, MA 01223
413-623-0202
www.carollew.com

CLASSIFIED CASE STUDIES
™
directly from the experts

#015 Old World Pet Portraits

It is a well-known fact that people love their pets, with billions of dollars spent each year on the health and care of these animals. Pet owners also like having photographs or portraits of their furry friends, as well. A decade ago, Carol Lew decided to find out if she could make a living as an artist. She combined her love of dogs, fine arts talent, and creativity and came up with an entirely unique idea: "portraits of dogs and cats dressed in historical costume," she said.

This was clearly a niche, and she needed to find other ways to sell her work beyond the traditional marketing in her local community. Her Web site, **www.carollew.com**, designed by her graphic designer husband, has since been a key element to building success, "though it's not usually the way people first discover my work," Lew said. First, she has to find other ways to get her name and artwork out in the world, such as word-of-mouth and leaving her business card with six examples of her paintings in appropriate places, such as with interior decorators, gift shops, and furniture stores. "I've been told many times that people make refrigerator magnets out of them," she said. That brings people to her Web site, "but without the site, there wouldn't have been a link to most of my potential clients," she said. The majority of her work is commissioned portraits.

"I use a number of methods to draw people to my Web site," said Lew, "such as licensing my artwork to a company who sold my prints internationally; painting exhibits in museums, upscale spas, galleries, or coffee shops in tourist towns; juried craft shows; local public and cable television shows; and newspaper articles." Naturally, her Web site address is on her card. She often gets calls from people who saved her card and eventually visited her site. Lew also makes prints of her favorite paintings. She has partnered with three other Web sites who sell pet-related items to promote these prints. When the Web sites receive an order, she drop ships the print to the customer, then bills the pet Web sites the wholesale price of the item plus shipping costs. Lew's Web site does not replace the need to market her business with traditional offline methods, but it is the best way, having the best of both worlds — online and offline.

#016 Pet Supply Store

Business overview

Pet owners want to purchase the best food and supplies for their pets, and even some unique items, such as clothing and personalized pooper-scoopers. Although this market is beginning to become saturated, you can still find some niches to attract pet lovers and turn this demand into a lucrative business. Many pet owners today are willing to spend whatever it takes for their pets. Your challenge is to narrow down the wide array of available products to a specialized item, which will keep your Web site user-friendly and focused on a particular niche. Some products, for example, are specially blended for different pet ailments, such as arthritis, diabetes, and heart and kidney problems. There are also natural foods for dogs, as well as birds, rabbits, hamsters, livestock, snakes, and lizards. You can also sell accessories, such as leashes and collars, cages, and toys. Spend your time thoroughly researching the online market and your competitors to determine what products will sell best. Drop shipping has greatly reduced the pet supply Web site owner's inventory costs. Many companies now manufacture and drop ship all-natural products, and others duplicate the raw-food diets of earlier years. Be careful: There are a number of dog supply companies asking for a monthly fee in return for a Web site and drop shipping orders. They promise that you can quickly launch your Web site and immediately start making money. But because you still must market your Web site, you are losing income from this monthly charge and spending time and money to advertise the company's product. Instead, go with one of the many drop ship firms not charging fees. Check with the different companies to see if they offer marketing assistance. The larger firms may suggest ways they can help promote your online business.

Skills needed

In this business, merchandising and marketing skills are a must.

Tips

Do not forget other animal products that are large sellers, such as fish aquariums, which can add to your income.

Look for pet toys that are different from the usual ones found in the stores. There is a wide variety of play items that the pet owners never see.

There has been considerable controversy about the quality of dog food. Be careful about the reputation of what you sell on your Web site.

Where to find more information

The American Pet Product's Association (**www.americanpetproducts. org**) is a not-for-profit trade organization consisting of more than 1,000 pet product manufacturers and their representatives, importers, and livestock suppliers.

Sideline Businesses

#017 Pet Boutique

There is designer clothing for men, women, children, and infants — why not for pets? If you are into fashion design and love animals, a pet boutique may be the business for you. There are many people who spend just as much money, if not more, on their pets as they do on themselves. They love buying pet attire, toys, and treats. Many owners now carry their dogs and cats in specially designed purses or expensive strollers, and make them look ravishing in rhinestone tiaras, pearl collars, and cashmere or faux-fur outfits. Luxury items can also include tuxedos, preppy and gothic pet collars, airplane dog beds, water beds, cat condominiums, and collectible toys. Dog owners also enjoy dressing their pets in sweaters and rain jackets, hats, boots, scarves, shirts, and even Halloween costumes. By finding a different approach or niche and becoming a blog and social network expert, you are bound to attract an audience for your fashion treasures. Plan marketing activities, such as inviting customers to send in photos of their pets wearing your products along with a drawing for a special prize for the best photo. If you make your own fashions, your prices will be based on your time and expenses. Otherwise, your price will be based on the cost of the company drop shipping your product.

#018 Dog Poop Scoopers

If you are interested in learning more about online niches, here is the scoop. You may want to create your own designer poop scooper, or become an affiliate of a store selling these products. What about biodegradable scoopers? They are easy to use and hygienic, and you can dispose of the poop in an environmentally friendly way. The materials of the pooper-scooper bag can be made from recycled paper and water-based inks. There are even plastic pooper bags that are totally biodegradable and compostable. With these products, cleaning up after pets is quick and easy. If the owner does not want to bend down to get the dog's waste, the dog owner holds a grabber with a biodegradable bag and rubber grip at the other end.

#019 Doghouses

Business overview

Want to help pet owners keep their dogs out of the wet and cold weather by living in a designer home? Many dog owners will gladly pay for a house in which their pet can be safe and warm. Although many people keep their dogs indoors, some dogs spend a great deal of time in an outdoor kennel and need to stay warm and dry. Your woodworking and architectural expertise can help dogs sleep in a stylish doghouse. You can design your own homes, or find a variety of different blue prints online. It is best to experiment with these doghouse plans at the beginning, unless you are an experienced builder. Most online doghouse businesses sell kits or traditional doghouses. You can definitely distinguish yourself with designer homes. With your saws, planes, sanders, nails, and paint, you can build log cabins, chateaus, or colonials for your clients' pets. Your work must be high-quality and unique, with different home styles and sizes for different types of dogs. If the owner asks you to custom design a house, perhaps to match his or her own home, you will need to see detailed and clear photographs. Once the house has been designed, get final approval from the customer before beginning to build it. Be careful on how you price your homes. Building these houses will take time, and shipping will not be cheap, so price the homes accordingly. Make arrangements to buy wholesale materials. Be sure to market your homes both off- and online.

Skills needed

You should feel comfortable working with tools, as well as communicating with customers about their wants.

Tips

Talk to a local veterinarian about how your house should be designed for the dog's safety and comfort.

If you are a woodworking hobbyist rather than a professional contractor, perfect your skills and products before launching your Web site. You want to be ready to meet your customers' needs as soon as you start marketing your business.

Where to find more information

Ron Hazelton's HouseCalls Web site (**www2.ronhazelton.com/archives/ howto/doghouse_construction.shtm**) offers step-by-step information on building dog houses.

Sideline Businesses

#020   Cat Litter Box

Do not forget the needs of cats. You can sell a variety of different cat litter boxes, litter, and assorted miscellaneous products. Or, you can create your own designer cat litter box. Most cat owners place their cat's litter box in an out-of-the-way spot to minimize odor and prevent litter from being tracked throughout the house. Now, you can sell designer cat boxes that look like wooden chests, except that they have an opening for the cat. The box is covered to hide the unsightly litter and contain the odor. Or, you may want to sell an automatic cat box that flushes the droppings away and cleans itself. The granules are washable, and the "toilet" connects to the water. If you would rather sell assorted cat products, you can find cat litter scoopers with a bacterial containment holder, so the owner never has contact with the litter.

CASE STUDY: BOBBI JO FORTE

Bobbi Jo Forte
President, Pet Commerce Direct
Animal Shelter Store
Germantown, NY 12526
1-888-723-8777
www.petcommercedirect.com

CLASSIFIED CASE STUDIES
directly from the experts

#021 Pet Commerce Direct

Pet Commerce Direct

When Bobbi Jo Forte was working in television production and public relations in 1997, her life was radically changed when she became a volunteer for a local animal rescue organization. "I saw firsthand how so many animals are abandoned, abused, neglected, or euthanized," she said, "and I vowed to devote my life to helping this cause in any possible way." In 2003, she rescued a severely debilitated and abused German shepherd named Chance. She recruited a team of experts to produce a natural remedy that greatly helped Chance's arthritis, and "By Vets Only" became a reality. She now sells this line at **www.byvetsonly.com** and continues to help thousands of dogs afflicted with joint-related problems such as arthritis and hip dysplasia.

Yet, Forte wanted to do more. Her main goal was to help shelters and rescues in their fundraising efforts through her personal e-commerce efforts. After spending a few years working with shelters and dog food distributors to get a sound foundation in the field, she launched two additional Web sites: the store **www.animalshelter.com** and the corporate site **www.petcommercedirect.com.** For purchases of food through 200 participating animal shelters or rescues, "I donate up to 25 percent of the profits to my customer's favorite organization," she said. Each participating animal shelter or affiliate also has a Web site with a banner about the program. Also, when customers shop at the Animal Shelter Store, they can split their purchase between their own pet and their favorite organization. Forte launched her sites in 2007 and made $36,000 the first year, strictly through organic (non-paid) marketing such as keywords.

Forte spends considerable time each day looking for additional dog food products for her site. She now deals with about 25 drop-ship companies that she handpicked because of their high-quality, made-in-USA product. She stays away from any firms with handling fees, and mostly works with smaller distributors. The drop shippers have a trial period, and Forte sets strict guidelines they must follow, like shipping the goods within three days. Each drop shipper is automated, so both she and the drop shipper can follow orders. "I know that much of my personal reputation rests on the products from my drop shippers," Forte said. "I can only expect that they share my highest quality goals."

#022   Homemade Dog Bones

Business overview

Dog devotees look to natural foods for the health and care of their pets. If you like to bake, and you also love dogs, think about starting a homemade online dog bakery. Natural treats and biscuits are in large demand. The business is particularly a good virtual venture for someone wants to work from home for very little investment. It is the perfect part-time business along with another part-time job, or to combine with a business selling other pet supplies. Pet lovers are beginning to carefully check the ingredients of their animal's food, becoming as interested in a natural approach for their pets as they are with other parts of their life. They do not like the large amount of additives and chemicals in commercial dog biscuits, and want their pets to live as long and healthy as possible. As a result, pet food is now more nutritious, and homemade dog biscuits are becoming popular with both canines and their owners. Even though there are already many businesses in this niche, there is still room to join the ranks due to the high demand. Most of the online businesses making these doggie bones have a unique spin; various flavors, shapes, and ingredients make one site different from the next. The ingredients are easy to find in a typical grocery store, and they do not take up a lot of room in the kitchen. They can also be simply packaged, and without much cost. All it takes is a recycled tin or paper, distinctive bow, and label with your clever business's name. You can make biscuits especially for dogs with diabetes or kidney problems, as well as high-grain, raw-vegetable, low-fat, and high-protein treats. If you have additional time, you can also sell bone packages at local stores. Develop a dog-lovers-centered Web site with up-to-date information, and perhaps even ways to donate to animal nonprofit organizations. Always be sure to focus on the needs of the dog owners and what is best for them. What about other pets? You can also make special natural snacks and foods for cats and birds. Why should these animals not eat gourmet, too? To get started, hand out free goodies at pet shows or expos.

Skills needed

This is the perfect online business if you love to bake and enjoy being creative. You will spend your time cooking up a storm and devising special marketing methods to increase sales.

Tips

You will need to check with the health department about producing and selling dog food out of your home.

Where to find more information

American Pets Products Association (**www.americanpetproducts.org**) is the largest non-profit trade organization for sellers of pet products.

Organic Pet Digest (**www.organic-pet-digest.com/dog-bone-recipes. html**) lists some dog bone recipes you can check out and try for yourself.

Sideline Businesses

#023 Dog Birthday Parties

Children have birthday parties — why not dogs? One of the latest on-line niches with a growing number of customers is a Web site offering dog party supplies. The dog celebration includes invitations, decorations, party-themed costumes, games (pin the tail on the cat?), and homemade doggie treats for a take-home favor. There are also online businesses supplying everything needed for a dog shower (mating and puppy arrival) and graduation from training school.

#024 Dog Cake

What is a dog party without a special cake made out of the canine's favorite food? Dog cakes can have layers of dog food and pepperoni sticks for candles. There are also bone candles, beef jerky bars, dog cake mixes, and chewies. You can either make cakes for your customers or sell cake mixes.

#025 Fly Tying

Business overview

If you love fishing and make your own special flies, fly tying may be a rewarding part-time income for you. The word "part-time" is important. To make $25,000 per year, you would need to make approximately 150 flies a year; however, if you make and price your product right, you can beat out the regular price and bring in some incremental income. Extra income is possible with related products, such as other fishing supplies. Fly tying is very popular, and there are many clubs and associations for fly-tying enthusiasts. If you have some experience with this craft and need a refresher, check around for continuing education classes. Or, take a lesson at a local fly-fishing shop or with another fishing enthusiast who has perfected his or her unique knack of tying. This will keep you from making expensive mistakes or, more importantly, investing in the wrong tools. It will also help you determine whether this is the right business for you. There are scores of pattern books, such as *The Orvis Fly Pattern Index* and Randy Stetzer's *The Best 1,000*. Fly-tying experts buy their materials through traditional sellers, but are also creative in finding other sources, such as road kill, hunters, furrier and tanners, and thrift shops. The object is to get the materials at a low cost in order to price your product lower than the competition. Typical varieties should be priced low, but if you have a specialty fly to offer, you can ask for considerably more money. Before starting your online business, spend at least six months tying every day, so you have a large inventory on opening day. During this time, set up a booth at local shows and give lessons on fly tying. Hand out your card with your Web site and the expected day of opening to start building a list of interested customers.

Skills needed

The more fly tying experience you have, the better.

You also need to enjoy repetitive tasks and have a great deal of patience.

Tips

To bring in additional income, sell books on fly tying and fly fishing, and become an affiliate for gift items and materials.

To stand out among other similar businesses, take requests from customers for customized flies.

Where to find more information

Fly Tying World (**http://flytyingworld.com**) is a valuable resource for beginners and experts.

Sideline Businesses

#026 Crickets

Crickets are a popular fishermen's bait and are always in demand. They can also be used as food for certain types of pets. The crickets are hatched and raised until they reach the correct size. They only eat mash and need clean water to drink, as well as a spotlessly clean place for the eggs to grow, hatch, and thrive. Brood crickets are sold somewhat higher than those used for bait. Crickets are very temperamental; they thrive at a temperature of 85 degrees — no more, no less. They are shipped in specially constructed boxes. This is a business that can be started on a small scale and then, over the years, expanded for a larger income.

#027 Worms

With the emphasis on going green, an interest in buying worms for composting is increasing. The worm is a natural garbage eater; when eating organic wastes, the worm places enriching nutrients back into the soil. The technical term for growing worms is "vermiculture." Gardeners use the worm's compost because it creates obvious positive results in plant and vegetable growth. They also buy live worms. You can actually start your own business by growing worms in your backyard, easily and inexpensively, and with little maintenance. It is possible to make considerable profits selling worms and compost, especially now that the demand for organically grown food has increased. You will need soil, and shipping and packaging materials for sending the product to customers. In the meantime, you are also building compost for your own garden with very low overhead costs. Use your Web site to "organically" market your worms, compost, and associated products.

Sideline Businesses

#028 Butterflies

When you look online under the words "butterflies for sale," a host of listings will come up for live monarchs for parties and celebrations. E-commerce business owners can also sell framed dried and exotic moths and butterflies. There is a substantial demand for butterflies from scientists, museums, private collectors, and laboratories throughout the world. There are approximately 20,000 butterfly species, and roughly 700 of these can be found in North America. You can import breeder butterflies from anywhere — as long as they are not endangered — raise them from the eggs, and sell the adults through the mail. Details about sending special mail (including butterflies) via USPS can be found at **www.usps.com/send/waystosendmail/extraservices/specialhandlingservice.htm**.

Chapter 11

Artists

#029 Web Site Designer

Business overview

When the World Wide Web was first established, there were only a handful of Web sites on the Internet. Now, there are Web sites of all types, from the most technically advanced to the simplest text-only sites. Today, there are more than 186 million Web sites available, and Web site designers are needed to assist with designing these sites for business and personal use. Today's Web designer has to do much more than design a Web site, though. In order to compete against other Web artists and template services, these designers need to offer an array of services, including SEO and incorporation of other elements, such as eye-catching video and sound, fast-loading pages, well-written copy, and a themed design that immediately gets the message to the viewer. You will work closely with customers and their marketing team to ensure your design fits with the overall company's business strategy. You may not only work on their Web site, but also be called on to help with other graphic design jobs, such as banner advertising, e-zines, and blogs.

Skilled needed

You need strong design skills, plus knowledge of programming and multi-media vehicles. You need to be familiar with SEO and writing Web copy.

Tips

You can charge either on an hourly or per project basis for your services. Check to see what other designers are charging and find a rate somewhere in the middle.

Where to find more information

The Web Design and Development Association (**www.wdda.org**) sets ethical standards and provides services to those in this field. Sites such as **www.elance.com** can be a source for frequent freelance jobs.

#030 Calligraphy Services

Business overview

If you have artistic skills and the mind of a writer/editor, a calligraphy service business may be a possible option. During the Middle Ages, monks used this form of writing in decorative books for the elite. Over the centuries, a wide variety of different print materials have been designed with calligraphy to add a decorative or formal look. Today, calligraphy is used for such items as wedding invitations, birth notices, family trees, and certificates of merit. With the advent of software programs, it is now possible to have computerized calligraphy that has the same look and feel as the "real thing." You may want to offer both handwritten and electronic calligraphy to make your business successful. Because of the competition in this field, offer a niche service. Carefully research the competition. Some businesses, especially those that have years of experience, continue to offer traditional calligraphy; they have built a clientele and reputation. Newer businesses offer silver or gold gilding; ribbons and other decorative items; special parchment and paper choices; added artistic elements, such as hand-painted flowers behind the written calligraphy; and a combination of both the traditional calligraphy and new software possibilities. Your Web site needs to clearly highlight what makes you different and show examples of your work. Even if you have to do several jobs for free, make sure you add testimonials to your site. Depending on where you plan on placing your emphasis — be it wedding invitations, unique designs for all special occasions, genealogy, or awards — make sure your Web site, domain name, and marketing are all in line with that specialty. You will charge different prices, depending on the difficulty of the work and the complexity of the assignment.

Skills needed

Even when using a software package that designs calligraphy, it is necessary to have a design or art experience. This business also requires someone who can handle last-minute changes and requests, especially with weddings and other special events.

Tips

With large orders, show a sample of the work before completing the entire job. Many times, people do not know what they want until they see an example of what they do *not* want.

For larger orders, create a contract for the services you will provide, a time-line for when the project will be completed, and the final cost (add in extras for late changes and design alterations).

You may be working on the same project for several months. In such cases, your contract should include at least a third of the money due upfront, and the remainder in two additional installments or upon completion. Do not wait until you have completed the service to be paid in full.

Where to find more information

Association for the Calligraphy Arts (**www.calligraphicarts.org**) is a non-profit for all people interested in fine lettering.

#031 Hand-Painted Tiles

Business overview

Homeowners who want a unique look for their house and appreciate creativity and artistic details frequently add custom, hand-painted tiles to their home décor. These tiles transform any nondescript area into a designer's delight. Most hand-painted tiles are customized based on the homeowner's specifications, so their color and design integrate well with the house's overall look. If you are creative and enjoy working in this medium, you may have your own specific style or offer a number of different designs, depending on the customer's needs. You may also be asked to reproduce an image or theme on the tile, rather than creating your own design. Or, it may be necessary to present the client with several different possibilities from which they can choose the final tiles. It may be that individual tiles come together to make a larger image. You will want to consult with the client to determine a style that will work best with their home's décor. The client should approve all colors and designs before you begin production. To determine what to charge for your artwork, check the prices of other established online tile-painting businesses.

Skills needed

In addition to artistic creativity, you should be able to see the larger picture. The tiles will look much different one-by-one as you are painting them than when applied to an area, such as a patio table.

Tips

Stay in touch with trends in home décor in order to provide your customers with the product they are looking for. Carefully check the quality of the tile before you buy in them in bulk from a wholesaler.

Where to find more information

How to Open & Operate a Financially Successful Painting, Faux Painting, or Mural Business, Atlantic Publishing Group, Inc. www.atlantic-pub.com.

#032 Handmade Wedding Invitations

Business overview

It is easy to order wedding invitations from a nearby stationery store or online. Yet most of these invitations have the same overall design and little originality. With the many types of handmade and recycled paper designs, there is no reason for this lack of creativity. You can help break this cycle by offering uniquely handmade invitations. With a little artistic creativity, there is no end to the ideas for creating wedding invitations. You can have specialized paper with pressed flowers, or beautiful recycled paper especially designed for invitations. The colors you use in the invitations should match those of the big event. Today's wedding invitations may include a variety of other items, including an initial "save the date" card and then a response card and stamped envelope, menu choice, directions, and/or invitation to an after-reception party or breakfast. Invitations today are just as eclectic as the couples themselves. Some of the invites are bright, bold colors with modern typeface and design; others are more traditional. You should work directly with the clients to ensure you have created a design they are happy with. Make sure you send the client a proof sample of the invitations before printing the entire set.

Skills needed

Brides are coming to you for a unique look and style, so it is important to be creative and design something completely different that matches the wedding color and theme.

Tips

It is often difficult for people to know whether they want a certain paper texture or color until seeing a sample. Make up small paper swatches to send to customers to aid their decision.

Where to find more information

Wedding invitations: A stylish bride's guide to simple, handmade wedding invitations, by Laura McFadden and April L. Paffrath

#033 Painted Clothing

Business overview

Do you have an artistic flair and enjoy fashion? At top-rated and judged craft shows, the hand-painted or silk-screened clothing booth is often the most popular, and these items are usually priced very high. Because you are selling online and do not have the overhead of a brick-and-mortar store or steep entrance fees to craft shows, you can sell your hand-painted clothing designs at a much more affordable and customer-attractive price. These designs are unique, and everyone loves that each outfit is one of a kind. You can make specially designed matching outfits for moms and daughters, older and younger siblings, and babies and toddlers. If sewing is not your area of expertise, order ready-made outfits from wholesalers who sell in smaller quantities, or team up with a friend who enjoys sewing. Use your artistic creativity to offer a wide range of available designs, such as large florals, angels, animals, Orientalia, abstracts, or geometrics. You may also sell different clothing styles and designs for varying historic periods, such as Victorian, 1920s, and 1950s. The more unique your creations, the better your opportunity will be to stand out from the competition. Conduct a thorough search online to see which hand-painted fashions are selling best. There are a wide variety of styles, materials, designs, and quality. You can paint on blouses, skirts, dresses, pants, blue jeans, and men's shirts.

Skills needed

In addition to being an artist, you need to have some experience in fabric painting and fashion in general. There are certain techniques that are important to know, depending on the material and paint used.

Tips

Offer a customized service, where you will paint a requested theme or color. You can have a different line of clothing, depending on the season.

Where to find more information

That's My Baby (**www.thatsmybabysstore.com**) is a perfect example of how to get started in this business.

Sideline Businesses

#034-041   Hand-Painted clothing

Below are examples of different options for creating hand-painted clothing.

- "Sock It to Me:" Hand-painted socks, no two pair alike
- "Name Game:" Cotton tops with the 1950s-style letter of first name
- "To a T:" Painted T-shirts or T-shirt dresses
- "Leg Go:" Tights and leggings colorfully decorated
- "Hand It to Me:" Old-fashioned women's gloves expertly painted

Sideline Businesses

- "Shoe In:" Painted tennis shoes
- "Tie One On:" Painted neckties
- "Tie-Dye:" Tie-dye clothing of all types

#042 Home Portraits

Business overview

Some artists have a special knack for painting from a photograph. Is that your specialty? What about painting or drawing home portraits? Many homeowners feel very attached to their houses and want hand-drawn or painted artwork of their abode to hang in the vestibule, or to pass down to the next generation as a family heirloom. Customers can send in photos of their childhood home, present family home, or a house of a friend they would like to give as a gift. These "homemade" works of art are perfect to give as gifts for special occasions, including Mother's Day, Christmas, or Chanukah, because they often evoke happy memories. Along with several photographs of different views of the house, the customer will need to tell you which architectural feature should be emphasized and what season to depict. Get a description of some any special additions you need to make to the photo that are not depicted in the photo, such as a cherry tree in bloom in the front yard during the spring or a decorated Christmas tree in the front window. You may want to offer suggestions on how to make the artwork different from the norm, such as painting four smaller draw-ings, one for each season, or the children and dog romping around the front yard. If it is a childhood home, perhaps the homeowner wants to include the family car during that time. Every house has a special character, and you can capture that for your customers with watercolor, oils, acrylics, graphite pencil, or pen and ink. Or, perhaps you have a mixed media you use that is different from the norm. You can also do other buildings, such as churches, schools, and businesses.

Skills needed

In addition to being a skilled artist in a specific media, you need to be able to capture the essence of a home from the customer's photograph and personal descriptions.

Tips

Ask the customer if there are certain colors that should be emphasized because of the décor where it will be hung. Also ask for a brief history of the house and the names of the family members. You can make a simple nameplate to go under the painting. Unless you charge considerably more, do not sell the portrait with a frame.

Where to find more information

Art and Home Portraits (**www.arthomeportraits.com**) is a perfect example of how to get started in this business.

Sideline Businesses

#043 Celebration Yard Signs

People often display yard signs announcing an arrival of a new baby, a marriage, or a birthday. With your artistic and wood-cutting abilities, you can create unique signs specializing in a specific niche market. People will always want to announce good news and let everyone else know what is happening. Instead of traditional signs displaying storks cut out of plywood, think of another way to jazz up these signs. It is important to create a unique but inexpensive way to compete, such as signs with multiple moving parts or lights. Experience or interest in art or design would be helpful, as would woodworking, set design, and painting skills.

#044   Scrapbooking

Business overview

Everyone wants to preserve their memories, but the hectic lives that many people lead prevents them from doing so. There are many different types of acid-free paper and supplies to jazz up personal photographs and memorabilia. Yet, all these supplies do not reduce the time it takes to actually complete the scrapbook. With a scrapbooking business, you can help individuals such as parents, grandparents, newlyweds, and sports stars put together their own special scrapbook. So many people have their photographs and other memorabilia thrown into drawers and boxes. They see other people's scrapbooks, where everything is put into order, and are envious, knowing they will never have the time — or perhaps the inclination — to do the same. A growing number of people have less time to scrapbook, but would like to have their old photos, children's drawings, and vacation souvenirs put into some kind of order. You should consult online, in person, or over the phone with your customers to choose the color and design of the overall book, and they should send you everything they want included. As another service, you can digitally scan, print, and archive the scrapbook for the client. You can also create template scrapbooks, which include a blank page design allowing customers to insert the photos themselves. In many cases, the photographs or other keepsakes can be quite brittle.

Skills needed

In this business, you should enjoy crafts, and be patient and methodical.

Tips

Instead of buying costly embellishments for the scrapbook, look around the house in your sewing area, children's rooms, and kitchen drawers for items to add to your scrapbook pages.

Only use paper that is acid- and lignin-free, and with a high archival quality and proper Ph level. This will protect the photos and scrapbook pages for years to come.

Where to find more information

Custom Scrapbooks by Ann (**www.customscrapbooksbyann.com**) is a perfect example of how to get started in this business.

Chapter 12

Business Services

#045 | Virtual Assistant Service

Business overview

One of the most popular services online provides businesses with virtual assistants (VAs), or the Internet's form of temporary workers. Companies use this extra help when they do not want to hire another full-time person, have a rush job to complete, need extra people to substitute for employees on vacation, or have work for a large, one-time project. As more small businesses are created that do not have a large number of employees, virtual assistants will become more worthwhile. As a virtual assistant, you can provide a wide range of help, such as making calls, setting appointments, bookkeeping, and transcribing tapes. There are a number of different ways you can charge for your services, such as hourly, per project, by the event, or on a retainer basis, where the customer pays a flat monthly fee. Once your business begins to take off, you can hire other VAs and take a percentage of the money they earn. It is best to develop a long-term relationship with clients, so they will contact you whenever the need for your services arises. Networking is the best way to spread the word about your new organization. Connect with companies to develop a list of on-going potential customers. Look for ads on such sites as **www.virtualassistantjobs.com**

when you first get started. Your Web site needs to list your specific services and testimonials from pleased customers.

Skills needed

In this business, you should be well-versed in word processing, technical writing, Internet marketing, networking, and sales. Business management experience, time management skills, and organization are big plusses in this field.

Tips

Becoming a member of the International Virtual Assistants Association and Association of Business Support Services — which provide certification, educational programs, consultation, and networking opportunities — is important.

Where to find more information

The International Virtual Assistants Association (**www.ivaa.org**) is committed to educating and certifying VAs.

#046 Transcription Services

Business overview

This is not to be confused with a medical transcription business. There are many other businesses that need to have work transcribed for such things as interviews, conference calls, market research and focus groups, radio shows, Webinars, and lectures. There are also a host of different types of organizations and individuals who need this service, such as authors who are conducting telephone interviews; government agencies that record meetings or have interviews with witnesses; insurance company adjustors who require an accurate recording of claims; nonprofit organizations who need meetings recorded; book publishers who tape editorial meetings; and life coaches, consultants, and speakers who record their presentations. You only need transcription equipment and a cassette player to start this business. Some companies requiring transcription services will hire workers with no experience, although the competition will be considerable for these assignments. It will be better to network with your local contacts first, as well as look online for freelance requests for transcription services. Because high-quality work with excellent spelling and grammar is required, be ready to take qualifying tests consisting of transcribing a short audio piece, as well as grammar and punctuation questions. Keep in mind: The speed at which you can complete a transcription assignment will depend on the audio quality; your familiarity with the subject; listening ability; and grammar, proofreading, and editing skills. You can find free typing, audio, grammar, and spelling tests online, or you can practice by transcribing podcasts on a wide variety of topics. You will normally charge per hour or by the project. In order to market your services, emphasize your strong command of the English language and grammar. If you are bilingual and can provide high-quality transcription in multiple languages, you are likely to receive even more projects.

Skills needed

Strong command of the English language. Good typing skills.

Tips

Some transcriptionists specialize in an area, such as real estate, and have a thorough knowledge of the terminology. Others market themselves as being able to transcribe a wide-variety of topics; if you decide to become a generalist, be sure that you acquire the necessary understanding of various business areas.

Where to find more information

The Medical Transcription Industry Association (**www.mtia.com**) is the world's largest association for medical transcription service organizations.

#047 | Translating and Interpreting Services

Business overview

Are you bilingual or trilingual? Do you know these languages grammatically as well as verbally? Do you like to write? As the world becomes more internationally connected, there is an increasing need for individuals to translate materials from one language to another, as well as edit information that has already been translated but has many mistakes. There are many online businesses that need help translating their Web copy from the native language into Spanish or English, or vice versa. You will be charging per hour or per project, depending on the client. Your marketing will consist of business-to-business (B2B) advertising. You want to reach out to Web site builders, graphic artists, and Web site publishers who may have customers who need your help. You also want to market to businesses that need two-way translation; for example, you can translate Japanese into English and English into Japanese.

Skills needed

Naturally, you need to be well-versed with the different languages. In addition, you must have good communication and selling skills, strong attention to detail, and be a stickler for deadlines and accuracy.

Tips

Advertise your services in trade journals and at business conventions. Make yourself known in business organizations on- and offline. Specialize in an area, such as blog writing, SEO articles, or press materials.

All companies have their own jargon, which is difficult to translate into other languages. When you start a new account, go over the copy carefully with your client to review such terminology.

Where to find more information

The American Translators Association (**www.atanet.org**) was established to promote the translation and interpretation professions and encourage professional development.

#048 Business Broker

Business overview

Business brokers, who also are known as business transfer agents or intermediaries, work with both buyers and sellers of small businesses to help with the procurement or sale of a business. These brokers normally confirm the business's worth, put it up for sale on a variety of outlets, interview potential buyers, accept quotes from prospective buyers, and negotiate the price for the sellers. Increasing numbers of people are interested in buying small businesses. Frequently, however, they do not have the expertise or the time to handle all the logistics involved with such transactions. They also do not want to make mistakes in the negotiation process, so they will turn to a professional business broker to assist with the process. Because business brokers spend all of their time selling businesses, they are well-versed in the process and remain up-to-date on the value of different enterprises available. A full-time business broker does not only understand the basics of business valuation, but also can call on a network of contacts. As a business broker, you may choose to list possible business opportunities on your Web site and charge these businesses a flat or monthly fee for being listed. You will advertise and promote your Web site through search engines and paid advertisements to draw interested parties to view this list. In this case, however, you are not actually pursuing business for the sellers. For a larger fee, you can actually make calls on behalf of the sellers and negotiate prices for them.

Skills

It is imperative to have the necessary business, sales, and legal background and experience to be this intermediary.

Tips

Become a Certified Business Intermediary through the International Business Broker Association to enhance your standing as a broker.

Where to find more information

The International Business Broker Association (**www.ibba.org**) operates entirely for the advantage of individuals and companies involved in the different aspects of business brokering, mergers, and acquisitions.

```
CASE STUDY:
MICHELLE L. LONG

Michelle L. Long, CPA, MBA
Long for Success, LLC
Lee's Summit, MO 64063
816-524-7799
www.LongforSuccess.com
```

#049 Long for Success

Michelle Long realized she had the experience and skill needed to publish her own book, given her background as a CPA, Founder, and CEO of Long for Success LLC; an MBA in entrepreneurship; an adjunct professor of strategic management at the University of Missouri - Kansas City; and a QuickBooks consultant and national trainer. As a result, she became one of the first authors to use Amazon's CreateSpace for self-publishing.

Her book, *Successful QuickBooks Consulting,* has proved successful, too, with approximately 3,000 sold within two years. "It's great." Long said, "Now that the book is listed on Amazon and my own Web site, I don't have to do anything but watch the royalties be direct-deposited into my bank account." Amazon handles the printing, mailing, and invoicing. She has also been pleased with CreateSpace's quality and customer service. Appropriately, Long has not solely relied on Amazon's marketing and promotion vehicles for selling her book. She uses the signature, "Author of..." in all her mailings, and comments on forums that are directly related to her book's topic. "I answer questions and give advice on the forums, rather than a hard sell, but they see my signature, and many may follow up and order the book," Long said. She is also promoting it through industry conferences and newsletters. "If you don't market," she stresses, "you will not sell."

Through Amazon's sales data, which is available through CreateSpace, Long can see that her best sales days are Tuesday, Wednesday, and Thursday, so these are the optimal days for posting on forums. She also has the first chapter of her book downloadable for free from her Web site. Long plans on writing additional books on QuickBooks because this has been such a successful niche. Her sales continue to grow with the support of Amazon: The better the book is in the rankings, the more it is displayed and recommended. This leads to more sales and a better ranking, and the cycle keeps going.

CASE STUDY: GARY NEALON

Gary Nealon, President
RTA Cabinet Store
641 Allendale Rd
King of Prussia, PA 19406
267-773-1006 www.rtacabinetstore.com

CLASSIFIED CASE STUDIES
directly from the experts

#050 RTA Cabinet Store

Carter Oosterhouse of HGTV's "Carter Can" invited Gary Nealon and Jake Park to his show.

Who would think homeowners and contractors would purchase kitchen and bathroom cabinets from an online wholesaler? According to Gary Nealon, **www.rtacabinet-store.com** sells approximately 2,500 "ready-to-assemble" solid wood cabinet sets a year to homeowners alone. In fact, after only two years of drop shipping cabinets, the primary distributor encouraged Nealon to get his own warehouse and start maintaining inventory because of the high volume of shipments RTA Cabinet Store was shipping.

Three years ago, Nealon was working in the logistics field as a director of sales and spoke with his friend's uncle who wanted help selling cabinets online. After testing out two sites, Nealon designed a Web site that, unlike some of the competitors, "makes it very easy for the customer to decide on the cabinet size and specifications," said Nealon. Customer service is a high priority. To help educate the end user, his company offers how-to videos and design templates, and even sends out samples so the customer can get a feel for the quality of the cabinets. Last year, he started a contest to reward the homeowner or contractor with the best story on purchasing, assembling, and installing the cabinetry for a kitchen renovation. The response was overwhelming, so this year, he upped the award to $4,000.

Nealon marketed the site organically, using keywords, hi
book, and articles on kitchen and bathroom renovations for promou
Web sites. "Education was most important," he said. "When you have a
new product online, you need to educate customers on what it means
to them." The site drew homeowners as well as contractors who were
looking for the best price and quality. They are now moving into a larger
scale of distribution by importing directly from China, and are working to
distribute into South America.

The growth of the business led Nealon to find an additional 25,000-square-
foot warehouse in King of Prussia, Pennsylvania, in addition to the main
distribution center in the Poconos. Further expansion includes researching other home improvement products and possibly outsourcing some
additional work to China. Not all home improvement products will be
able to be sold online, due to the difficulty of shipping some items, but
Nealon sees the home improvement market moving more toward an e-
commerce platform as homeowners and builders become comfortable
purchasing supplies online.

#051 | Telephone Answering Service

Business overview

One of the easiest home-based businesses to start is a telephone answering
service. The income generated depends on the size of the business and the
services available. Even with the new electronic technologies, businesses
still rely on the phone. A well-run answering service provides personal
communication that is crucial in today's economic situation. Relying on
voicemail may lose potential customers and makes a business appear very
impersonal; there is also no guarantee the caller will leave a message. Sometimes, if a customer receives an automated response, they will go on to the
next company offering the same services. When someone calls with a specific need or question, a real person should respond and provide information. Potential customers are businesses needing an answering service who
are "on call" around the clock, such as health care providers, repair services,
and utility companies. This business may be difficult to operate individu-

ally, especially if you have multiple clients. You may take calls as the actual business, or as the answering service.

Skills needed

A pleasant voice and excellent communication skills are critical. You must have the ability to multitask and not become stressed when needing to respond to several people at a time.

Tips

If you are able, offer bilingual services, which will widen your list of potential customers. Do not take on more businesses than you can comfortably handle. You do not want to put people on hold for long periods of time.

Where to find more information

The Association of TeleServices International (**www.atsi.org**) was established in 1942 to enhance the members' advancement through education, certification, and awards programs.

#052 Online Publicist/Public Relations

Business overview

Brick-and-mortar businesses and other traditional organizations have long used public relations (PR) professionals to spread the word about a company's positive image and brand. Now that businesses are online, the PR plays the same role, but does not use the same media. For example, in the past, press releases were primarily sent to print publications, such as newspapers and magazines. Now, with online businesses, most of the PR is electronic. Regardless, PR continues to be an important part of the marketing equation. Your job may include traveling and juggling of assignments and meetings. If you are just breaking into the communication field, do whatever you can to build your portfolio. This may mean handling PR for a low cost, or free for the first few months. Online PR consists of activities meant to influence the media, social networks, and online users who are primarily using the Internet for their communication and commerce needs. On behalf of your client, you will interface with blogs, forums, search engines, press release distribution services, e-zine article placement sites, and social networks to promote their business. You will also be concerned with brand reputation. To disseminate your client's news, you will use vehicles such as press releases, wire services such as PR Newswire and PRWeb, an Internet media kit, and an excellent SEO campaign. You will be very concerned with keywords and ranking high among search engines. The final goal, of course, is to get people to come to your client's Web site with positive feelings about the product or service. Check with other PR professionals to determine the going rate to charge per hour, or on a retainer basis.

Skills needed

Excellent writing and research skills; the ability to conduct interviews and meet strict deadlines; strong communication skills; and the desire to network with others.

Tips

Consistency is the name of the game in online coverage. You need to set aside a specific time every day to write and send out articles, blogs, and e-mails for your clients. Another time must be devoted to telephone calls.

Always remember those keywords in everything you write. That will keep your press releases on top of the search engine list.

Do not use the same copy when submitting to several blogs and press release services; the search engines do not like repetition. Make enough changes that it appears to be a different article.

Where to find more information

The purpose of the Public Relations Society of America (**www.prsa.org**) was to advance the profession and the professional.

Sideline Businesses

#053-055 Public Relations

Below are variations on the publicist or public relations professional:

- **Artist's agent**: This person may work with gallery owners and private art collectors who are seeking a particular style of art. This person nurtures the artist's talent, offers advice on his or her future direction, finds the artist future work, and negotiates business contracts.

- **Photographer's agent:** This individual builds his or her client's customer base with new assignments and gallery exhibits, and continues to establish existing relationships.

- **Author's agent**: This person assists the writer with publishing a book or other literary work, and negotiates advances and publishing contracts to their client's best advantage.

#056 Freelance Proofreader

Business overview

Whether it is in print or on the Web, people are needed to make sure published information is error-free. Proofreaders are the last to see the printed or electronic copy before it is published. Editing and proofreading are not the same: Editors look at the written work to ensure that it flows and is coherent; however, it is the proofreader who gives the final check for formatting, spelling of names, and any errors or omissions. Proofreading requires a person who is very thorough and a stickler for consistency and accuracy. You will work with printers, book and magazine publishers, and

Web producers, and read such materials as reports, brochures, annual reports, and Web sites. Most proofreaders are paid by the hour, unless they are working on a per-project basis. The majority of publishers are looking for people who have had some experience in proofreading. To get work, you will need to establish relationships with editors, copywriters, and publishers, and make connections with online proofreading organizations, forums, and blogs. You may have to start with small, low-paying jobs in the beginning. However, this is a networking, "who-you-know" field. Contact everyone you know and everyone they know, and never be afraid to take even small jobs to gain experience. If you have an editorial background and do not have experience in proofreading, you may have to do some work for free with volunteer organizations or new Web sites. In many cases, you will be given a proofreading test before you are hired for a job. You must be well-versed in proofreading marks for hard copy and know all the most popular manuals of style, such as APA, MLA, and Chicago. For electronic copy, you will be making changes on the screen. There are no standards for electronic proofreading, so you will either define them for yourself or determine if the client has already defined their standards.

Skills needed

Strong writing skills. Extensive knowledge of English grammar and spelling.

Tips

Specialize in a specific area, such as medical proofreading or technical proofreading. If you know another language other than English, this can be helpful in finding additional work.

Where to find more information

The Editorial Freelancers Association (**www.the-efa.org**) is a nonprofit resource for editorial specialists and those who hire them. Sites such as **www.elance.com** can offer a source for frequent freelance jobs.

CASE STUDY:
TINA MCALLISTER

Tina McAllister, Owner
Beyond the Pen, LLC
2030 W. Baseline Rd, Suite 182-232
Phoenix, AZ 85041
602-684-5007 www.beyondthepen.com

#057 Beyond the Pen

Successful online businesses are continually finding that information is the key. Blogs include interesting items on a topic that link back to a Web business's products or services. Articles on submission sites target specific populations of readers and draw them to an online business. E-books or e-reports establish and build credibility and relationships with present and potential buyers. "Online business owners need to realize that everyone knows something — has an expertise in a subject — that is of interest to someone else," said Tina McAllister, who provides writing and editorial support to e-commerce sites.

With all the time spent on product development, sales, and marketing, it is difficult for many Web store merchants to find the time, and often the inclination, for writing. McAllister launched her online communication business, BeyondThePen, last year, after 15 years of writing materials for offline businesses. "I had been dabbling in online communication with ghostwriting e-books, and saw the extensive need for someone to help others develop their own online business books and articles," McAllister said.

As a freelance writer, ghostwriter, and writing coach, McAllister has written both print and electronic books, articles, Web copy, and press materials for busy professionals in various industries. Recently, McAllister has been spending more time on e-book coaching, as she recognized many businesses want to write an e-book or report, yet do not know where or how to begin.

Wearing her coaching hat, she works closely with home businesses that want to build their online presence with written communication. She helps them look at all phases of the e-book development, which includes determining the purpose of the book, establishing a topic based on the particular business or service, defining what material will be covered, writing an outline, and formatting the final text.

McAllister has also written her own e-books for the work-at-home business owner, including some on her expertise of real estate, and plans on writing many more. She is taking her own advice on the importance of providing information online. "Any online business, especially one that provides editorial services as mine, should be writing e-reports and e-books," McAllister said. "These electronic publications are so viral, because everyone is looking for information, and are such a wonderful way to build ongoing trust with customers."

Sideline Businesses

#058 Research Service

Both online and traditional publications need researchers to track down information and confirm facts and figures. Companies use researchers to put together packages on competing businesses, consumer trends, and the industry marketplace for strategic plans. This business used to be called information brokering, but changed with the arrival of the Internet. As a research service, you collect data and facts that are relevant to a specific subject(s), then sell this information to individuals and businesses. Companies also hire the services of an online researcher to find specific data and facts relevant to their particular business, industry, or market. A good researcher is creative and knows where to find information beyond the typical sources.

Sideline Businesses

#059 Fact-Checker

A fact-checker makes sure a publication is printing factually correct information and does not include information that will result in a lawsuit. A fact-checker's aim is not to locate new information, like a researcher, but to confirm the value of the information at hand. Fact-checkers normally have some legal experience, or can at least look at copy with an eye to the legal aspects, and double-check the content's validity, authenticity, and legitimacy. They may also have a background in library science. Publishers, businesses, and freelance writers use fact-checkers to approve represented information. Working as a fact-checker can be a good work-at-home job. There is a lot of flexibility, but there can also be important deadlines.

Chapter 13

Parents and Children

#060 Disposable Diaper Service

Business overview

Parents often must run out of the house to get diapers, which can be very inconvenient. Diaper services sell and deliver name-brand diapers to parents all over the country. No more waiting in line and spending a lot of money at local convenience stores; now, you can easily order diapers from the convenience of your own home. You can also sell wipes, formula, shampoos, salves and ointments, breast pads, and powders. You want to make sure you offer the best name brands at the lowest price, with low or free shipping and fast delivery. Top customer service is a must: These moms and dads will not wait on hold or deal with a late delivery. New parents are used to being catered to, and they will gladly spread the word to their friends and acquaintances if they are pleased with your Web site. This typically young group is familiar with Internet communication, so be sure they can find your business on social networking sites, instant message services, and blogs. By offering tips and parenting advice through Twitter, YouTube, and your blog, customers are likely to view you as an expert in your niche, thus choosing your products over the competition. Any other plusses you can offer them, such as downloadable coupons, diaper club discounts, and opportunities to chat with other parents, will be a big plus.

Skills needed

You should be familiar with current social networking venues and "green" product trends.

Tips

Make it worth your customers' while to stay with you month after month: The more they buy, the lower the price.

Where to find more information

The Real Diaper Association (**www.realdiaperassociation.org**) provides support and education to parents all across the United States for the use of simple, reusable cloth diapers.

Sideline Businesses

#061   Online Cloth Diaper Service

This is a business you can establish for a particular geographical area and expand over time to additional cities. Advertise online and off. When someone signs up for your services, you will drop off cotton diapers to that customer twice each week. At the same time, you pick up the used diapers from the previous deliveries. These may be left outside the door. These diapers do not need to be cleaned or even dunked; you will bring the diapers to a professional laundry service that emphasizes cleaning for sensitive skin. Your services can also include laundry bags and pins.

Sideline Businesses

#062 Adult Disposable Diaper Service

Although not a children's service, it is becoming an increasingly large market due to the changing age in population and may make a logical addition to your children's diaper service. A growing number of adults individuals need to purchase disposable diapers on a regular basis due to medical reasons or aging, as well as being disabled. You can provide this service by working with a drop ship company. You can also sell associated items, such as bed pads, garment liners, and skin care lotions.

CASE STUDY: SARAH MASCI

Sarah Masci
Owner, Lullaboards, BabyLuxe {daily},
Paperluxe Studio, and D'luxe Press &
Design, North Carolina
704- 968-4565
http://lullaboards.com

#063 Lullaboards

How can someone succeed on the Internet? You name the way, and someone is probably doing it. Sarah Masci, for example, is using several entrepreneurial approaches to find a happy medium between staying at home with her children and being a two-income family. She continues to work part-time in energy management, but meanwhile is building her e-commerce presence.

Masci recently developed her own product, Lullaboards, sold at **http://lullaboards.com**, from personal experience. She has a nanny who comes a few times a week to help with her sons, ages 2 and 4 (with a third on the way). At the end of the day, there are always several questions that Masci, like most parents, will ask childcare providers. "Rather than a paper report, I decided it would be better (and less wasteful of paper) to have a dry-erase system for reporting on my children's day," said Masci, "where the caregiver just writes with a dry-erase marker." The Lullaboard can hang easily from the refrigerator door, or be slipped into the daycare bag.

Masci also makes incremental income through the advertisements on her blog, **http://babyluxedaily.com**, which provides Masci's insights on how to find great buys based on her former baby boutique ownership. She also retails through **http://paperluxestudio.com** by offering personalized stationery for women that can be given in lieu of traditional party favors at events such as baby and bridal showers. Then, she provides services with her partner, Dana Blake, at **www.dluxepressand-design.com** for public relations and graphic design for children product manufacturers. Masci literally and figuratively has her hands full with all these online ventures and her personal life, but she is proving that the Internet is for the imaginative entrepreneur.

#064 Baby Hands and Footprints

Business overview

The Internet is saturated with hand- and footprint kits for babies, so why not find a new way to make a memorable gift for moms and dads that will remind them of how small their bundle of joy was at birth? By looking at some of the other clever options online, you may be able to come up with a unique offering of your own. A newborn, especially the first one, is a special arrival whom parents want to remember forever. The time goes by so quickly and it is sometimes difficult to remember just how small that precious baby boy or girl was at birth. Because of this, many parents and grandparents enjoy hand- or footprint plaster kits. Because this market has become so saturated, you will need to find a new niche for this market. Once you have your new idea, market your product to Web sites for expecting and new parents, and baby shower and baby gift blogs.

Skills needed

Creativity is important here because you have to come up with a new approach for a long-loved tradition. Excellent marketing skills are critical.

Tips

Remember that sometimes the name of a product is just as important as the product itself.

Where to find more information

Casting Keepsakes (**www.castingkeepsakes.com**) is an excellent example of how to start this type of business.

CASE STUDY: KYNA WOOLLERY

Kyna Woollery
Micah & Co.
Post Office Box 932
Horn Lake, MS 38637
1-866-423-7559
www.micahco.com

CLASSIFIED CASE STUDIES
TM
directly from the experts

#065   Micah & Co.

Anyone who starts an online business and plans for it to be successful soon knows it is not only a great deal of work, but also a large and quick learning curve. Kyna Woollery, a part-time speech therapist, decided to build an e-commerce site, **www.micahco.com**, to have more time to spend with her daughter, Micah. Woollery's small hometown only carried traditional baby products, so she often had to drive to larger cities that had a larger selection.

She realized that many other women had this same difficulty, and decided that her Web store would offer boutique quality baby items to order from the comfort of home. In addition to her boutique products, she also offers personalized baby blankets, baby shower invitations and favors, and a free baby registry. The latter gives moms-to-be who sign up with Micah & Co. 50 cards to let friends and family know she is registered here for baby gifts. This baby registry is also one of the many ways that Woollery learned to build her site and opt-in customers.

When Woollery decided to open Micah & Co., "everything was new," she said. "I had to take a crash course. I spent hours and hours researching the Internet for information on how to start an online business." Then, with the help of women in a Yahoo! mother's group, she built her Web site from an established template and Web host, and "poured my heart and soul into my work," she said. Finding drop-ship companies that were 100-percent reliable and ethical was her next challenge. One year later, finding additional drop-ship firms continues to take a great deal of time: "Some drop shippers enclose blind invoices and use their own label on the packaging, so Micah customers would only see their brand name, not mine. That greatly reduces my chance for repeat customers." She also warns e-commerce people like herself that some drop-ship companies actually steal the names of the Web store's customers for their own marketing purposes.

Since the baby product business is so competitive, marketing is a very high priority for Woollery, so she is always scouring the Internet for additional suppliers. "There are always new products coming on the market that can keep my Web site updated, fresh, and 'ever green,'" she said. One year since Woollery decided to go online, her business continues to grow, and so does her knowledge. She has found that starting a Web store is a learning experience that never ends.

#066 Handmade Children's Gifts

Business overview

There is always a market for unique or customized gifts for children. These can include clothing, hats, keepsake boxes, pillows, and wall art. The product is up to your own creativity and ability. In this type of business, you can sell a range of products, such as baby blankets and bibs, girl's dresses and bonnets, boy's T-shirts and leather caps, and girls and boy's toys — kites and puppets, for example. Or, specialize the products with a particular theme, such as ballet outfits, sleepwear, scrapbook covers, toddler cloth toys, or T-shirts. Because this market is already saturated, it is important to find a niche that children enjoy and that lends itself to handmade items. Choose a product that can be produced with the highest quality, but does not take too much time or labor to produce. Your Web site will need to be designed to fit the theme of your product, and you need to carefully photograph each item with a child wearing or using the item.

Skills needed

Being crafty or skilled in carpentry can be a plus in this business. You must also be creative enough to find a niche for this business.

Tips

The "tween" and teen market is huge, but there are few handmade products for this age group. If you have a teen at home, see what items may be of interest, such as purses, backpacks, or iPod covers.

Where to find more information

Polka Dot Patch Boutique (**www.polkadotpatch.com**) is an excellent example of how to get started in this business.

#067 Handmade Children's Toys

Business overview

Are you a kid at heart who appreciates the value of handmade products, wants to work on your own, and has skill in woodworking or sewing? Many parents today are leery of cheap and poorly made foreign toys, and green or homemade toys are increasing in popularity. Consider producing a toy you enjoy making or loved having as a child. Parents are usually looking for a toy that is well-made, can entertain and educate at the same time, and can be played with over and over again. If you are a "crafty" person who works well with a jigsaw, you may want to consider making simple learning puzzles with vibrant colors and train sets, boats, or board games for older children. Research your ideas to make sure the niche is not already saturated. Your marketing strategy should include a blog about the history of toys and other information of similar interest, and social marketing related to the benefits of your toys and how they work. Also stress that they are made in the United States. Remember that customers buying from this niche expect quality — not only in the toy itself, but also in the toy's packaging and instructions. Customer service is also essential. Anything you can do to make your customers' lives easier is necessary. This will give them more time to play — with their children and your toys!

Skills needed

Excellent customer service is essential in this business. You must be creative enough to design a unique niche.

Tips

Your toys should be similar to vintage toys, but should be updated for the modern child. For example, rather than making the traditional wooden truck, design a three-dimensional truck puzzle with 15 easy-to-handle pieces. Rather than producing a train, design a three-stage rocket. Regularly test your products to ensure they meet U.S. regulatory safety standards.

Where to find more information

Wee Little Sprouts (**www.weelittlesprouts.com**) is an excellent example of how to get started in this business.

Sideline Businesses

#068   Sock Puppets

A sock puppet is a children's toy dating back to the 1920s. Online, you can find "do-it-yourself" sock puppet instructions, and some toy stores sell handmade or commercial sock puppets. These puppets are greatly enjoyed by children and are used frequently with storytelling. Brainstorm new niche avenues for selling sock puppets. If you are a writer, design characters to go along with a short children's book you have written. Or, you can sell kits for making sock puppets at home. Craft tools, such as a glue gun, make it easy to produce puppets.

#069   Handcrafted Children's Playhouse

Business overview

Children have a great imagination, and many parents are now buying handcrafted playhouses for their younger children. Although constructing these homes takes a great deal of skill and time, they can become a very profitable business. If you have the architectural and woodworking ability to put stylish homes together, you can make creative and elaborate playhouses. Many homes are built to look just like the family's house in order to enhance role-playing. Have customers can send you a photograph in order to recreate their home. If you trained as an architect, you can design your own homes. To develop a niche, build playhouses that resemble other structures, such as rockets, ice cream parlors, castles, or cars. Purchase the supplies and tools you need through a wholesaler to keep your costs low. The size and construction of the house will depend on whether the house is used indoors or outdoors. The latter should be made to withstand weather. Sometimes playhouses connect to swing sets. With your creativity and expertise, no matter if the house is indoors or out, the children will feel right at home.

Skills needed

You must be handy with tools and also familiar with computer design software to create blueprints of your playhouses.

Tips

Market to an upscale customer base that can afford these types of high-end products. Do not use substandard materials that lower the overall quality of your house.

Where to find more information

Kids Crooked House (**www.kidscrookedhouse.com**) offers a great example of how you can start a business from your love of carpentry.

#069   Childcare Finder

Business overview

Single parents, two-income parents, traveling executives, and busy families often need babysitters, nannies, and emergency caregivers when children get sick. There are many parents who do not have necessary child care and want a cost-effective way to locate help when needed. But the traditional way of finding care is quickly becoming outdated. Neighborhood teenagers are sometimes unreliable and not often trained in CPR and first aid. The online sites offering child care matching services often have several thousand subscribers who are looking for some form of child care. In order to attract a wide audience, you will want to offer a variety of different types of caregivers. Your Web site should include a database of caregivers and the families requiring care. Both the caregivers and families will need to set up a profile about themselves. The caregivers should include references. You cannot be responsible for conducting a security check on each person or family registered, and you should make customers aware that they need to check the provider's references before hiring them. Consider placing an advertisement on your site for a company offering background screenings, and offer customers a discount for using this service. Also provide sample interview questions for both caregivers and families to determine if the match is right. Your site will offer a free preview of available caregivers, but you will charge a monthly or yearly fee to register and access specific information on the babysitters and nannies. Parents should be able to pay upfront with a credit card, and this will free you from needing to handle billing and collections. Some Web sites offer free services to both the providers and the parents and are, instead, paid through advertisers on their Web site. Most of your subscribers will learn about your business through search engines and word-of-mouth.

Skills needed

You should be somewhat Internet-savvy, because you will have to work on the Web site and spend your time marketing.

Tips

Keep an even number of caregivers and parents registered on the site. If one side gets too large, market heavily to the other side.

Although you will not be screening individuals, you need to make it easy for the users to do so. Provide templates of caregiver profiles, including a place for qualifications and references, which can be downloaded from your site. Also warn babysitters not to give away bank account or social security numbers until they screen the families. There are scams on both sides of the equation.

Another option for this business is to make additional income by charging advertisers to appear on your site. Many Web sites offering services such as this make an income in this manner. Advertisers will pay big bucks to advertise on a site that attracts a large number of customers. Market to advertisers that relate to the area of business you are covering.

Where to find more information

The International Nanny's Association (**www.nanny.org**) serves as an overarching organization for the in-home child care industry and provides information, education, and support to consumers and industry professionals.

#071   Tutoring Services

Business overview

Students have more scholastic demands placed on them than ever, especially with a growing emphasis on testing and the need for a college degree. Many students fall behind and need educational assistance their school cannot provide, thus online tutors are becoming more prevalent. If you are an educator, a tutoring service is an effective way to make additional income. As an online tutor, you will set up a specific time when you and the student will conduct lessons through instant messaging and Internet communication services such as Skype. There is also Web-based software you can use, as well as online "white boards," where both of you can interact in real time. You will need to decide on a specific subject or subjects in which to tutor students, based on the needs of the student and your expertise. You should specialize in one or two similar areas, for example geometry and algebra. You do not need a license to tutor, but of course the customer will check for your educational credentials. It is also necessary to define your target market — whether it is elementary school, middle school, high school, university, or adult students. Your rates will most likely be hourly, unless a student needs extensive help and you are put on retainer. In order to market your availability, put ads on Craigslist (**www.craigslist.org**), or create a MySpace or other social media profile to appeal to a young audience. Mention that you offer a special, such a free half-hour of tutoring, or a free e-book. Market locally offline as well. Submit a press release both to print and electronic media outlets, or partner with local schools.

Skills needed

You should be have teaching experience and be licensed in your state to teach the subject you are offering.

Tips

You will make more money if you are hired for an extended period of time. After the free half-hour session, discuss future tutoring needs.

Once the student begins attending sessions on a regular basis, keep in contact with the parents. Set aside a regular to discuss the student's progress.

Another option for this business is make additional income by charging advertisers to appear on your site. Many Web sites offering services such as this make an income in this manner. Advertisers will pay big bucks to advertise on a site that attracts a large number of customers. Market to advertisers that relate to the area of business you are covering.

Where to find more information

The International Tutoring Association (**www.itatutor.org**) gives members an opportunity to share with others in the field.

#072 College Planning Services

Business overview

There are many aspects to consider when making a decision on which college or university to attend. With so many possible schools, the concern with which major to choose, and the looming financial questions, it is not an easy process. In current economic concerns, it is more important than ever to find schools offering the best financial package. A college planner can help give student the personal attention they need to make the right choice. College admissions experts have experience in counseling, plan development, and financial aid. They are great researchers and solution providers. If you already have this experience, starting an online college planning service may be a great fit; otherwise, you will need do a great deal of research to get to know the ins and outs of the industry. You will help high school students and their parents weigh the pros and cons of each school and counsel them on how to find the best fit. It will be helpful for you to design or use a skills/needs assessment to match the needs of the students and parents with their school options. Once the students have narrowed down the list, they may need help filling out applications and other forms, setting up a calendar with specific due dates, writing their application or scholarship essay, and negotiating the best financial package. You may need to make phone calls to the schools to gather more information and get dates. Because of your special skills and knowledge on what colleges expect in an application, you are acting as the student's personal marketing agent. Some college consultants specialize in a certain type of school; for example, Ivy League universities, community colleges, or private institutions. Normally, you will charge clients on a project basis, or have fees for different services offered.

Skills needed

A thorough knowledge of the colleges and universities, admission procedures, and financial aid alternatives is essential. Strong research and communication skills are also necessary, as are contacts at a large number of institutions.

Tips

If you have not visited a large number of colleges, plan on spending several months doing so. You should visit at least 35 or 40 universities in your area to determine their areas of expertise. Online research is important, but does not compare to actually visiting the school first hand.

If you have an education background, take a business course to learn necessary business skills.

The public is often warned to verify the credentials of college admissions service providers, so a certification in the field and references are important.

Where to find more information

The Independent Educational Consultants Association (**www.education-alconsulting.org**) is a 30-year-old organization for educational placement advisors in private practice.

Chapter 14

Clothing

#073 Clothing Store

Business overview

To keep costs low, you will need to personally design and make your own clothing, or use a drop-ship company. By using a drop shipper, you will not need to keep the clothing in stock at your location. The drop shipper should include your return addresses on the shipment, so customers are unaware you are not inventorying and sending the shipments yourself. You can choose from hundreds of suppliers, large and small, who sell everything you want — from socks to evening gowns. Make sure you carefully choose your drop shipper, and evaluate and test your suppliers. As with other businesses, you should establish a niche, rather than carry a broad range of clothing. SEO is an important aspect of this type of business. If you are selling clothing for women over 5'11," for example, your Web site should contain those keywords.

Skills needed

Business and marketing skills are just as important as fashion experience. If you are less knowledgeable on these subjects, consider taking a few courses at your local community college.

Tips

Experience in the retail industry, preferably with clothing, is important.

Where to find more information

Apparel Search (**www.apparelsearch.com**) is an online information source and guide to the apparel and textile industry that offers help for industry professionals and assistance with their daily questions and needs.

Sideline Businesses

#074   Vintage Clothing

Vintage clothing is a niche that people either love or hate, which makes it perfect for an online store. Selling this type of clothing online allows customers who love this product find items they cannot usually find in stores. If you are considering starting an online vintage clothing store, you most likely are already wearing or selling these items. You will have to expand your hunt considerably to build a large inventory. This will require many trips to thrift stores and estate sales for clothing from the 1960s, 1970s, and 1980s. Talk with estate sale firms and stores than may have clothing they cannot sell. Market your Web site on MySpace, StumbleUpon, Hoobly, and TheThriftShopper.com.

#075   Handmade and Vintage Aprons

In the 1920s and 1930s, feed sacks were often used as aprons to prevent waste. A couple of decades later, these aprons became very fashionable, and many different designs were available. The real aprons or handmade replicas continue to be popular. Web sites selling these aprons have discovered a lucrative niche. Stores sell reversible aprons, customized aprons, aprons for the whole family, and gardening or carpentry aprons. If you decide you want to sell the real thing, you can usually find them at antique stores. Consider combining the old and the new by adding new decorations or vintage jewelry to the older apron, making your products unique.

Sideline Businesses

#076 Handmade Baby Items

In the past, many older women would knit or crochet sweaters, booties, and blankets for newborn babies. Many of these items were so well made they could passed down from one generation to the next. If you enjoy knitting, crocheting, or sewing, consider making homemade baby clothes, blankets, and bibs. There is also a market for handmade quilts and wall hangings. Baby clothing takes very little fabric, and the clothing styles are usually consistent. You may end up smocking or making personalized baby pillows or handmade diaper bags.

#077 Traditional Dance Costumes

If you are an expert seamstress, as well as a creative designer, you may want to go into the costume business. Belly dancing costumes are often requested. These elaborate costumes — which include a veil, bra, skirt, and harem pants, as well as accessories — are frequently decorated with intricate beadwork, sequins, and fringe. Each one is unique, and they can range from $25 to several hundred dollars. You can also sell finger zills, or cymbals, which are used in this type of dancing. Another popular dance costume is the Egyptian dancing horse, which tells the story of the country's equestrian history. Other dance accessories that can be sold include coin anklets with toe rings and coin belts, ringing hand bracelets, coin bras, oriental and Egyptian necklaces, and dance shoes. Similar costumes and accessories are also requested for other nationalities.

#078 Costume Exchange Service

Dance costumes (for ballet, tap, or jazz recitals) are costly expenses for parents. Many children are unable to attend dance classes because of the cost of the costumes for their recitals. Consider starting a costume exchange service, connecting parents who have costumes that are no longer needed with parents who have a child in an upcoming recital. You can also connect dance studios with other dance instructors who may have a need for a large number of similar costumes.

Sideline Businesses

#079 Dance Tutus

Ballet continues to be a favorite interest for young girls, and handmade dance tutus are often needed for recitals, or just for playing dress-up. You can custom design these ballerina costumes and dress-up creations, or feature a selection on your Web site. As with the belly dancing, you can sell the accessories as well, such as slippers, silk flower tiaras, jeweled tiaras, hair adornments, and leotards. These are perfect for Halloween, birthday parties, and everyday play.

#080 Formal Children's Dresses (for pageants or weddings)

Formalwear is needed for young girls for such occasions as wedding or pageants. Fashionable dresses are also worn on Easter and Christmas, for portraits, or other memorable times. Handcrafted dresses are even more special, especially when both mother and daughter lend their interests and suggestions to the creative process. If you are an expert seamstress, consider starting a Web site offering handmade formal dresses made from materials such as organza, tulles, velvet, satin, and silk, with a close attention to detail. Young girls love full twirling skirts, lively colors, big bows, and intricate trims. Your creativity and skill can provide a dress just as beautiful as one made by a designer at a much more economical price.

#081 Homemade Doll Clothing

In every generation, new dolls become popular, like the American Girl series, which became a marketing phenomenon. The American Girl Web site reports that approximately 14 million American Girl dolls were purchased since 1986. Approximately 620,000 girls are subscribers to the monthly American Girl magazine. American Girl clothes can be quite expensive, with a pair of pajamas priced at $25. A lucrative business can be made if you can sew or knit these clothes and accessories and sell them at a price covering your time and expenses — and beats the American Girl prices.

CASE STUDY:
JOSEPH TANTILLO

Joseph Tantillo, President and CEO
Greekgear
6 Commerce Drive, Freeburg, IL 62243
(618) 539-9998 www.greekgear.com

#082   Greekgear

"Niche" is an important word for e-commerce. When merchants are fortunate enough to find a niche that sells, they are not only able to grow the original Web site, but can spin off "niches of the niche," so to speak.

In 1999, Joseph Tantillo, president and CEO of Greekgear, found his niche starting an online business specializing in fraternity and sorority clothing. Since then, Tantillo has grown his "niche" idea into a $3 million business with 20 employees, 4 million customers, and more than 15 different sites. Tantillo initially sent out all production, but soon learned that purchasing his own equipment was the key to keeping up with demand, controlling costs, and better serving his customers.

"We grow about 30 percent per year and are always trying new ways to expand," Tantillo said. For example, this past year he saw competition mounting and his growth slowing down, so he invested in changes to his Web design and organization: "The Web site is where it all starts, and a place in which we have to continually stay focused." With that said, growth is back to normal. Tantillo, as with other successful e-merchants, emphasizes that a site does not just grow by itself. "Owning a Yahoo! store is not just a hobby to do in one's spare time. If you really want to be successful, you have to make it happen," he said.

Tantillo added that "you need to have a positive attitude and keep trying new things. Even at down times, it is necessary to do research on ways to build the business." He sees the Internet as a way that anyone, regardless of background, can succeed. "It's a great equalizer. And, it's a great way to quickly see the results of your efforts. By making a change for the better on my site, I can see almost immediate results."

Some of the fraternity and sorority Greek-related sites are:
www.greekgear.com
www.sigmachigear.com
www.tkegear.com
www.sigmaalphaepsilongear.com
www.thetachistore.com
www.greekpages.com
www.divineninegreek.com

Tantillo has also expanded his niche concept to other markets in which people are passionate — from their nationality, with Italian-based Web site **www.guidogear.com**, to people's spiritual faith, with the popular Web site **www.christiangear.com**, and even to dog lovers, with **www.gearforgoldens.com**. Tantillo's goal is to open a new niche Web site every year. Considering he has nearly 20 Web sites to date, he is way ahead of schedule.

CASE STUDY: KATHY AND DAVE WOJTCZAK

Kathy and Dave Wojtczak, Owners
Element Jewelry and Accessories
www.elementjewelry.com

#083   Element Jewelry and Accessories

Kathy and Dave Wojtczak, owners of Element Jewelry & Accessories, opened a retail jewelry store in downtown Seattle in 2004. They soon found that high rent and other expenses kept them struggling to stay afloat as a brick-and-mortar store. In 2005, they signed up to sell their jewelry on Amazon Marketplace. A year later, they added their own branded Web site, **www.elementjewelry.com,** as part of Amazon's WebStore program.

They had so much success selling on Amazon that when the store's lease was up in 2007, they decided to leave the world of physical retail behind. "Now, I manage our business from home. Customers can shop 24 hours a day, 365 days a year, while I have the freedom to work when

I want from where I want," Kathy said. "I have been able to spend more time with my family, and even take a few vacations."

How does the couple sell in such a competitive category as jewelry? They are able to keep their prices competitive, because they no longer have the overhead and operating costs associated with selling in a physical store; they said that they were able to pass those savings on to customers while still maintaining a good profit margin. That simple concept has actually changed everything. Before Kathy came to Amazon, her daily life was much different: "I worked in our store nine hours a day, six days a week, 52 weeks a year. In-store traffic was unpredictable, advertising was expensive, and store-related overhead was outrageous," she said.

In June 2005, Kathy uploaded about 100 items and started to watch the sales come in. She had two sales in June, so she added more inventory. She had 39 sales in September and kept going. In December, she had more than 200 sales. "Within six months, I knew that the growth potential from Amazon far exceeded the growth potential for my physical store," she said. She and her husband now offer more than 2,500 items on their Web site, and they are still growing. "This year our goal is to double our selection and double our sales from last year," said Kathy.

Sideline Businesses

#084 Niche Jewelry

The online market is saturated with traditional jewelry. But people are also interested in nontraditional and new styles of jewelry that are not regularly seen. With your knowledge of beads and bangles — and your creativity — you can discover a unique type of niche jewelry that will drive people to your site. The important word here is "unique." You need to sell unusual yet high-quality jewelry differentiating you from the thousands of other jewelry sellers. You can make your own jewelry fashions or drop ship them from jewelry vendors. Either way, you work to determine your target market and what type of jewelry these individuals will want. Your product must match the audience; your Web site must have detailed and high-resolution photographs.

Chapter 15

Collectibles

#085 | Antiques

Business overview

Are you a collector? Perhaps you would like to sell your special collectibles to other people who have similar interests. With an antique Web site, you could sell antique kitchen utensils, sports memorabilia, or Disney items. As you know, people collect everything from elephant figurines and buttons to old personal computers. It will be necessary to find a niche with a balance between the bizarre and the generic in order for this business to be lucrative. Research items in collectible guides in print and online, or talk to dealers at antique shows and flea markets. Once you decide on your niche, look at the prices for these items online on other antique collectible marketplaces and Web sites to set your prices. Take photographs of your items and specify any information you know about the item, including size, date, material, where it was purchased (and by whom), and whether it has a signature by the creator of the item. You also need to list the condition from good to "as is," as well as signs of wear, such as scratches, chips, dents, corrosion, stains, mold, writing, refurbished parts, or tears. You will need to keep your collectibles in a safe area of your home or office that is away from children and pets and well-ventilated. Do not store items in the heat or near an air conditioner. Keep a detailed inventory list of each item you have in your home, as well as any collateral pieces, such as covers. Make sure your homeowner's insurance will cover these items in case they are stolen or destroyed.

Skills needed

You need to be well-organized, and you must enjoy the hunt. You will be spending a great deal of your time looking for items to add to your collection.

Tips

Search for specific items you do not have, but that your customers will want. One of your largest costs may be packaging and shipping, depending on the size, fragility, and packaging difficulty of your item. Before you set your prices, determine these packing costs.

Where to find more information

The North American Collectible Association (**www.nacacollectors.com**) supports dealers and serious collectors of all forms of collectibles.

#086 Auctions

Business overview

Ebay has enjoyed much success because people love a good deal and the feeling when they simply believe they are getting a good one. Even at a regular auction, it takes just two bidders to keep the action going strong — each wanting the item, or wanting the other person not to get it. Although the auction business is highly competitive online, there is still room for those with the right niche. Find a niche that is not already saturated with businesses, but has a lot of prospective bidders. Some of the most popular Web sites auction antiques, collectibles, and artwork. You can auction vacations, sports tickets, clothing, rare books, or anything you have expertise or knowledge in. If auctioning sites are not your forte, try a different business model. Instead, consider starting a bartering or trading site, or a site that provides the opportunity to swap vacation home properties. You will need computer software designed for auction services, and you will receive a commission on each item sold. Some sites charge the sellers a fee for registering. Another option for this business is make additional income by charging advertisers to appear on your site. Many Web sites offering services such as this make an income in this manner. Advertisers will pay substantially to advertise on a site that attracts a large number of customers, so market to advertisers that relate to the area of business you are covering.

Skills needed

You should feel comfortable about online software. Because you will spend a great deal of your time hunting down and signing up auction vendors, the same traits that make salespeople successful will help you, such as communication, patience, fortitude, and organizational abilities.

Tips

Consider joint venturing with other Web site owners who have already built lists of potential bidders. You would get less of a commission on the sales, but have a ready market. Or, find out if you can add an auction to a Web site that sells related items.

Where to find more information

The National Auctioneers Association (**www.auctioneers.org**) provides education and programming for this industry.

#087 Used Books

Business overview

Despite the fact that one of the largest companies online is Amazon.com, and it makes substantial income from used books sales, many other Internet-based used bookstores are making a sizeable profit. If you have a knack for hunting and finding desirable nonfiction books and — most recently — academic textbooks, it is still possible to do quite well in this sector. This business is perfect for someone willing to scrounge through boxes, basements, and attics for products to sell. You must also be dedicated to keeping up-to-date with the changing needs of the buyers and the books they desire. Books are not difficult to find; however, books selling for double or triple the original price are generally more difficult to locate. By partnering with Amazon, you can get regular updates on top-desired items. It will be necessary to establish several different ways of acquiring books, such as garage sales, library sales, thrift shops, and local Goodwill and Salvation Army stores. You can also search the Internet for used books, and manufacturer or wholesale closeouts. You can sell your books directly through your Web site and/or through **www.amazon.com, www.abebooks.com, www. alibris.com,** and **www.biblio.com**, where you will have greater competition and be forced to pay a commission on your sales, or a fee to the company. Selling books is a detailed business requiring computer software to track your personal inventory, items for sale, and items that have ordered, billed, and shipped. You will also need a place to store and package your inventory. It is also possible to use companies such as Amazon to inventory, package, and ship your books.

Skills needed

This is a business that takes strong business skills, as well as a love of books. You will be spending a great deal of your time searching for books and growing your business.

Tips

Stick with selling nonfiction books, unless you can find first-edition, signed fiction books. Fiction books are usually very common and cannot be sold for more than a few dollars.

Where to find more information

Book Sale Finder (**http://booksalefinder.com**) offers a complete guide to book sale events and the book selling business.

Sideline Businesses

#088   Rare Books

Some used booksellers do not sell rare books, and many rare book dealers do not sell used books. Millions of books have been published, but only a very small portion of these are thought of as rare. A book is only rare when its demand exceeds the supply. Books can be considered rare because of their contents, design, or physical makeup. They can be first editions of important literary works, historical events, or scientific inventions. They may be illustrated with valued works of art or photographs, or they may be only one of several copies in existence. Scarcity is often a reason for a book to be desired. Research books using services such as **www.bookfinder.com** to determine the worth based on the number of copies presently for sale and the value to collectors. The age of the book, however, does not make it valuable. It can be a newer book that is scarce, or an older book that is not desirable. You will find that certain categories — such as all books before 1500, English books prior to 1640, and American books prior to 1800 — will be of interest.

Sideline Businesses

#089 Book Closeouts

Each year, bookstores have thousands of books, graphic novels, and other print materials that go unsold. These remainders can be a sideline to a used-book business, or be sold separately online. With this business, you will purchase books in large quantity, instead of individually. Before you buy, you should be aware of which will sell. Check the book's sales rank on Amazon to determine their retail cost; otherwise, you will be stuck with the remainders of the remainders. You can buy these books online from remainder businesses or wholesalers for approximately 20 percent of the original cost. Know exactly what you are buying. Do not buy skids, or pallets, of books for a low cost, as many of them may not sell.

#090 Textbooks

Used textbook sales are becoming increasingly popular among booksellers. College students are looking online for textbooks to avoid the high costs associated with buying new textbooks from their university bookstores. Market your Web site to this group. When listing textbooks on your site, be sure to note the edition, as new additions are released frequently, and students need to buy the edition their professors have requested.

Chapter 16
Consulting

Consultants are found in almost all areas of interest. A consultant is a person who shares his or her expertise with others, and thus has greater skills, training, and knowledge in a particular area of study. This person is not only an effective learner, but also an effective instructor and trainer. Consultants usually charge by the hour, by the project, or on a retainer basis. If you have a specific area of expertise, you can use your Web site to market your knowledge to those in need of the information.

Below are some examples of consultants with businesses online. Some consultants do all their consulting through the Internet, by phone, or through e-mail. Others use their Web site to market their business and will meet with clients in person or over the phone. Each of the areas of consulting require their own particular educational backgrounds, training, and prior experience. Many of these businesses cannot be started without first having the necessary training.

#091 Feng Shui Consultant

A person who is knowledgeable in feng shui, or "wind and water" in Chinese, advises people on how they relate to their surrounding environment. They help clients alter their homes or working environments to be more physically, mentally, and emotionally balanced and healthy. These consultants visit with clients either on-site or online through a floor plan, and they provide a written and visual report with their recommendations. A degree in or previous experience in interior design can give you a boost.

#092 Color Consultant

Colors make people react in different ways; a blue room, for example, is cool and soothing. Many professionals and businesses acquire the advice of color consultants to determine which colors to use on packaging, paint next year's line of cars, use for an upcoming fashion design, or utilize for the inside of a restaurant. Color consultants have the experience and innate ability to discern among different hues, and they know how they will influence the intended audience. Having a degree or previous experience in interior design is often useful.

#093 Disability Consultant

The impact a serious illness or injury has on one's ability to return to work is the major focus of disability consultants, who have the training and experience to read and analyze medical treatment records. It is possible to determine functional impact and medical limitations in a job analysis/ disability evaluation report for a long-term disability application. If you have a degree or previous experience in medicine or human resources, it will be beneficial.

#094 Government Contract Consultant

With increasing financial constraints, it is becoming necessary for many businesses to seek additional funds through government contracts. However, it is difficult to find one's way through this maze of red tape and detailed policies and procedures. Government contract consultants specialize in working with firms presently looking for or conducting business with federal, state, or local government agencies, helping them meet the stringent requirements properly and effectively. Success in this field may require a degree or previous experience in technical writing or political science.

#095 Graphologist or Handwriting Consultant

In the past, a handwriting consultant would provide insights into an individual's personality through a signature. Some employers continue to use graphologists for this reason. Also, with the advent of computers and scanners, it is has become much easier to forge signatures on checks and legal documents. Graphologists are hired by corporations, insurance companies, law firms, and financial institutions to determine the validity of a signature and are hired to appear as witnesses in court. A degree or previous experience in criminal justice or communications is often needed.

#096 Health Insurance Consultant

It has become increasingly difficult for people to find health insurance they can afford that adequately covers themselves and their families. In many cases, adequate insurance is available, but many insurance policies come with numerous different options and language that is difficult to decipher. An insurance consultant has knowledge in the field, and strong Internet and telephone research skills. This expert does not represent any one insurance company, but rather is hired to find the best match for his or her client's needs. To be successful in this area of consulting, you may want to obtain a degree or previous experience in the medical arena.

#097 Homeschooling Consultant

With the varying quality of education nationwide, many parents have decided to homeschool their children, and many children are homeschooled because of religious or health reasons. But parents may not have the background and training to develop the required curriculum, and need the advice of a homeschooling consultant to evaluate the student's educational needs, develop a curriculum, give examinations, and communicate with an advisory school on a regular basis. You will need either a degree in education or experience in the teaching field for this business. Previous homeschooling experience is also advisable.

#098 International Business Consultant

Technology, especially the Internet, is making the world smaller; it is easier than ever to communicate with someone from another country. Meanwhile, every country is becoming more diverse in its population. Numerous companies are forming joint ventures or starting ventures in different nations, but this may be difficult due to language and cultural differences. The international business consultant provides information about foreign business investment opportunities, competition, practices, and legalities, and will work as a liaison between two or more businesses that are forming an alliance. A business consultant may also research options for an individual or company wishing to establish a joint venture with a party in another country. To be successful in this area of consulting, one may need a degree or previous experience in business or international relations.

#099 Nutrition Consultant

It is well-known that a person's health can be dependent on nutrition. Many people are unhealthy due to the foods they eat and a lack of healthy vitamins and nutrients. There are also those who have a particular illness requiring a routine diet. Hospitals, health clubs, corporations, and individuals hire nutrition consultants to recommend a meal and exercise plan, as well as to provide personal encouragement. You might want a degree or previous experience in nutritional science before considering this area.

#100 Online Fundraising Consultant

Fundraising consultants develop programs to help nonprofit organizations increase donations and other forms of contributions. The Internet provides additional avenues for fund development; it is now possible to use social networking, e-mails, Web sites specifically geared toward causes, and "donate now" buttons. This field is expected to continue to grow as more nonprofits expand their efforts online to use e-philanthropy. A degree or previous experience in business or nonprofit management may be helpful.

#101 Web Site Consultant

Individuals who are not Internet-savvy, but know what they could successfully sell online, often use the services of a Web site consultant to develop a business plan, create a Web site, set specific goals and how to achieve them, and market and launch the venture. They contact this person regularly with ongoing questions and concerns until they have a better understanding of how to operate their businesses. Success in this area of consulting may require a degree or previous experience in information technology or the graphic arts.

#102 Credit Counselor

People commonly abuse their credit cards. With the steep interest rates that go along with this abuse, they may find they can never pay off what they owe. Each month, they are paying the interest rather than the principal. The amount continues to grow, and the credit card holder continues to get further and further behind in payments. It is not long before creditors begin to call, because it becomes difficult to pay all that is owed each month. As a credit counselor, you will help clients who are overextended financially. If you have a degree or previous experience in finance, you may be especially able to have success in this field.

#103 | Life Coach

Do you have a background in social work, psychology, or a related field? You may want to become a life coach to help others set and reach their goals. This is different than a psychologist or counselor. You are not helping the person cope with emotional concerns; rather, you are helping the client define what they want to achieve either in the short- or long term and set a specific plan to reach this goal. You will set a specific time(s) to converse with the client each week over the phone or computer.

#104 | Weight Loss Consultant

Not everyone can join a health club or become a member of weight loss program and stick to the guidelines. Many do not have the motivation, and may jump from one type of diet to another. A weight loss consultant works with individuals, developing customized meal plans and, more importantly, setting goals and following-up with the client on a regular basis to chart progress. If you have a degree or previous experience in nutritional science, this is an area to consider.

CASE STUDY:
KATHERINE CONNER

Katherine Conner, Owner
RX MEDS PARTNER
54 North Lake Circle
Manning, SC 29102 1-866-655-0838

#105 RX Meds Partner

RX Meds Partner
Your RX Benefit Savings Source

One of the exciting aspects of the Web is that new types of businesses can be created as service needs arise, such as handling the red tape and complexity of the U.S. health care system. Katherine Conner's mother was only receiving $612 a month from social security when she had a stroke, and her doctor prescribed $600 worth of medication. Conner said, "I immediately started Googling for help, but found there was very little information online from the government or private Web sites on how to pay for this medicine." After three months of research, with her and her brother carrying the load of medication costs, Conner finally found patient assistance programs that offered free pharmaceuticals. Recognizing how many others were struggling with this same situation, Conner donned a "Patient Advocate" hat and started **www.RXMedsPartner.com**.

Conner shares information on her Web site that allows patients to find out if they qualify for free medication and other health care programs. The Web site is subscription-based: Patients fill out a short eligibility form and are shown a database listing all the free and discounted medication programs to which they can apply. "When patients determine they are qualified for free medicine, they answer some questions, and our database system fills out all the necessary applications. The patient can print the applications right at home or at the library, and they get all the information needed to apply. If their doctor changes or adds medications, they can research a free program for that medication and update their records in their member control panel online, 24/7," Conner said. Web site members receive timed reminder e-mails for refills and other free resources, such as discount coupons for prescription and over-the-counter pharmaceuticals, rebates, and the newest health and financial assistance programs.

It is clearly recognized that a niche Web site is a proven way to become an online success. Yet, it may take more time to build a clientele if the product or service is new. Conner said one of her biggest challenges is "getting people to believe they can actually get something this valuable free." She has also accepted affiliates so others can offer her service, and continues to market, build, and grow her business. Conner realizes that expanding her Web site will be a slow process, but believes the benefits are well-worth it.

Every day she hears from people who cannot afford their medication, such as the mother of five with lupus and Attention Deficit Hyperactivity Disorder who could no longer write and was struggling minute-by-minute to survive. "In 15 minutes, I found all but one of her long list of medications free. She told me that with the savings, she could now afford important testing to monitor her conditions that she had [previously] not been able to afford. It is truly satisfying to see my patients' lives change in such a positive way."

Chapter 17

Crafts

#106 | Unusual Yarns

Business overview

Are you an avid knitter? Do you make your own yarn? There are many knitting lovers who would be interested in the latest yarn additions and/or patterns. There are many different types of yarn, such as luxurious alpaca, cashmere, organic cotton, lace, beaded silk, and even hand-painted. If you are a seasoned knitter, you probably have your own unique types of yarn, or you may like to try new yarn whenever possible. You can purchase products from yarn suppliers throughout the world, and sell the newest and best yarn available. Although the traditional way of making yarn is spinning separate fibers together into yarn on a wheel — which you may do yourself — there are many other ways of creating special handcrafted yarns. Many yarns are popular with knitters because they blend different textures and hues. For example, it is possible to blend a mixture of mohair, cashmere, silk, merino, and bouclé to produce a textured look. Other knitters have one-of-a-kind yarns that come with additions, such as beads or stones.

Skills needed

In this business, you should either be a long-time knitter and or yarn-maker. Creativity and knowing the ins and outs of your target market is important.

Tips

Knitters often like to actually see and feel the yarn before they purchase it. Offer samples to customers if requested. If you can make a long-term faithful customer by sending out one snail-mail envelope, then do it. If you cater to the knitters who always want to try something new, consider a yarn-of-the-month club, or a "secret bag" with mixed unknown goodies. You may be able to learn to make yarn through leisure classes at your local college or adult center for a low cost.

Where to find more information

The Knitting Guild Association (**www.tkga.com**) is a nonprofit community committed especially to knitting and knitters.

Sideline Businesses

#107 Eco-Friendly/Green Yarn

Organic yarn is a new trend in the business. Because this area is still very new, you should be able to market to an entirely different group of people, either with your yarns or with products made with organic materials. These yarns — made directly from plants such as bamboo, animal-derived materials, or a combination (such as soy-silk) — use a special procedure for washing and spinning with a vegetable base rather than petroleum soaps and oils. They do not have chemical dyes or bleaches. This does not mean, however, that they are bland. Natural colors come in a wide array of bright colors. For the real green lovers, recycled polyester yarn, produced out of post-consumer and post-industrial waste, is also available. Bamboo yarn is similar to the soft and silky ramie for a smooth, flowing look.

#108 | Handmade Candles

Business overview

Candles for special occasions and those for home decoration, scent, and romance are very popular items. Handmade candles can be specially made for customers. Candle making can also be a profitable business if you have a high-quality product with a variety of oils and perfumes. Because this is a competitive market, you should immediately define your target audience. When you begin your candle-making business, it will be helpful to sell only a few specialized products. You can narrow your specialty by the ingredients used, scents available, or techniques used to make the candles, such soy candles, votive candles, or painted candles. Your marketing efforts will depend on the type of candle you decide to create. For example, if you make beeswax candles, you will be marketing to people who appreciate natural products. If, however, you make aromatherapy candles, you are targeting individuals who practice alternative health. In addition, you can have a competitive edge by using the highest-grade wax and fragrance. Although you can purchase cheaper ingredients, the candle will not burn well, or the fragrance will not be long-lasting. You do not have to purchase top-of-the-line candle-making equipment, but find out what equipment has a good rating with other candle makers. In some cases, your packaging will be just as important as the candles themselves, because this is what customers see first when receiving your product. Labeling and a professional-looking presentation of your business logo with contact information is essential.

Skills needed

Even if you have been making candles as a hobby, make sure you have the additional information to make safe products for consumers. Spend a great deal of time experimenting and refining until you have candles that meet the highest quality standards.

Tips

Call your insurance agent and check into liability insurance in case a faulty wick sparks a fire in a customer's home. Also discuss necessary labeling for safety precautions. Many people go into candle making without properly testing their materials; they do not recognize the danger these candles present if not made properly. Because these candles will be in homes, it is imperative they are made safely.

Where to find more information

The Handmade Candle Co. (**www.handmadecandles.com**) offers a great example of how you can take your craft and turn it into a business.

Sideline Businesses

#109   Soap Making

In the past, soap was made with lye and animal fat, was difficult to produce, and was quite odorous. Those days are gone. With a proven recipe of ingredients, you can make soap right in your kitchen. Today, with an emphasis on "going green," people want natural, handmade soaps for themselves and for gifts. Many people find ingredients in store-bought cleansing goods questionable; they want simpler and more wholesome products for skin care. You can also sell similar products to these same customers, such as scented candles. The scents, colors, and shapes are what make your soaps memorable. Your customers will be looking for a variety of different type of soap, such as goat's milk, oatmeal, and hypoallergenic varieties. Order the best soap products on the market to keep your quality high. Once you have your soaps perfected, give thought to ways that you can reduce time and labor and still keep the quality. You can reduce costs by buying in bulk or establishing a good relationship with one supplier.

Sideline Businesses

#110 Homemade Bath Products

Many Web sites are doing quite well financially by selling easy-to-make handmade bathing products. If you have an interest in following or developing recipes for bath and body care, you could possibly start a business selling your products. Bath products are very popular, and buyers are looking for a wide variety of fragrant gels, bubbles, soaps, and scrubs, as well as bath accessories such as loofahs, scrubbers, and slippers. You can develop your own formulas, or find recipes online. This is also a product you can easily sell offline through craft or home shows. To widen your selection, sell other natural items, such as aromatherapy bath salts, body lotions, and hand creams. Consider your options for making and storing your products. Check with your town hall for licensing regulations, and with an insurance agent regarding liability coverage. Purchase your ingredients from wholesalers in bulk shipments to lower costs.

CASE STUDY: BILL ASKENBURG

Bill Askenburg, Proprietor
New England Birdhouse
800-815-0062
www.newenglandbirdhouse.com

CLASSIFIED CASE STUDIES
directly from the experts

#111 New England Birdhouse

When Bill Askenburg and his family moved to New England in 2001, he decided to leave his full-time advertising and marketing work and become a stay-at-home dad. Pursuing his interest in woodworking and backyard birding, Askenburg built a birdhouse that was an exact replica of his family's new home as an anniversary gift for his wife. His wife was not only thrilled by the gift, but also suggested he make others for neighbors and her coworkers. The gifts were a hit, so Askenburg followed his wife's recommendation and began to sell custom birdhouses online. Two months after building his own Web site and advertising it with Google AdWords, he got his first sale. Since then, Askenburg has been building these $1,200 - $1,600 custom birdhouses on a continual basis. "Who would have thought?" he said.

Although these houses have been giving him steady work, about five years ago Askenburg decided to take the next step and open an online storefront, selling stock replica birdhouses, backyard birding supplies, patio and garden décor, and unique New England-style artisan items on his site. This would add incremental income during the months it took him to make each custom birdhouse. Askenburg did not want to go with just any e-commerce shopping cart template, since he had a particular idea of how he wanted the Web site to look: wanting it to reflect the custom, handcrafted, and regional attributes of his brand. Another difficulty was finding the right firm to handle the cataloging, fulfillment, shopping cart, payments, and customer service. He was pleased to find the National Catalog Association (NCA) out of Southbury, Connecticut, that specializes in this area. "NCA gives me a reasonably priced, turn-key online storefront solution, manages my back-room, and lets me focus on growing my business," said Askenburg.

To minimize overhead expenses, Askenburg did not want to keep his own inventory, so he looked into drop shipping. Now, he partners with more than 15 different companies that sell drop-ship products, and he features the works of other New England artists. Askenburg sees drop shipping as a "no brainer." There is no overhead, and he can expand his business in phases. He spends several hours a week scouring the Internet for products that his customers would want to buy. Askenburg describes his customers as "backyard birders," or people who like seeing and feeding birds in their garden or patio and appreciate hand-crafted and unique, regional artisan wares. "Knowing your customer demographics and their interests, shopping needs, likes, and dislikes is critical," he said.

Askenburg stays clear of so-called "top drop-ship company lists," opting instead to establish direct relationships with firms for his inventory, because he has found that "many of the company lists are fraudulent." Instead, after finding a product that would appeal to his customers, he contacts the company, usually by e-mail, to gauge their interest in drop shipping. Askenburg primarily searches for small businesses and artists in the New England area and said that promoting other regional businesses is a priority for him. Many of these are smaller firms and do not charge a drop ship or handling fee. He has not found it difficult to find reputable companies that drop ship, as it is now becoming a commonplace practice for small e-commerce sites. Rather, the challenge is expanding a site's product line without becoming too broad. "The more specific the product line, the better," Askenburg said. "To be successful, New England Birdhouse has to stay true to its niche, and only offer products that our backyard birder will love."

Chapter 18

Employment

#112 Career Counselor/Coaching

Business overview

Do you have experience in the field of social work, theology, psychology, education, human resources, or another related area? Online career counselors provide career advice and help clients target career decisions in telephone conferences. They analyze and evaluate their clients' personal interests, skills, volunteer activities, personality traits, educational background, and employment history. Many also provide support with looking for a job, writing a résumé, and preparing for interviews. Career counselors may also offer guidance to those who are presently working but unhappy with their jobs. A major part of a career counselor's role is providing support to those who are undergoing a major transition, suffering job stress, or dealing with a lost job. In such cases, the career counselor may suggest a career interest test, which matches personality traits and abilities with employment avenues. The end goal is helping the clients determine their future direction in their career life. Another option for this business is make additional income by charging advertisers to appear on your site. Many Web sites offering services such as this make an income in this manner. Advertisers will pay to advertise on a site that attracts a large number of customers, so be sure to market to advertisers that relate to this field.

Skills needed

A background and interest in counseling, where your strengths include listening, being objective, lending support, and providing clarity on issues.

Tips

Before starting your own career counseling Web site, you may want to work with one of the larger online firms and learn the ins and outs of the business. Also check to see if any of these companies have an affiliate program.

Consider a niche in this area, such as women transitioning into the job force after raising children; people transitioning from sports into traditional careers; or middle-age men and women who are searching for a completely new direction.

There are many programs online offering a career-counseling certificate in a few weeks or a few months of education and training. Check these out carefully and make sure they are certified.

Where to find more information

The National Career Development Association (**www.ncda.org**), which helps people define their careers over their lifetime, is a division of the American Counseling Association.

Sideline Businesses

#113   Senior Employment Services

Many baby boomers will not retire at the traditional age of 65 because of better health and exercise, increased cost of living, and higher living standards. In addition, health care costs and the desire to keep busy encourages seniors to remain in the workforce. Thus, an increasing number of online businesses are beginning to cater specifically to this population. Many employment sites for the 55+ demographic are popping up on the Web. Your Web site could list jobs available for this older demographic. It could also have a wide variety of articles geared specifically to help these candidates search for and find work. Many of them have not looked for work in years or possibly decades, so your Web site can also provide an opportunity for employers to target this older population. You can generate income in a variety of ways: You can charge employers to place ads on your site, or candidates to post their résumés. You can also offer services, such as résumé and cover letter writing, coaching, and personality career testing.

Sideline Businesses

#114   Résumé Service

In the past, writing a résumé was not difficult. The résumé included personal information and a simple description of the candidate's position, company name, and responsibilities. But today, with an employer looking at hundreds of résumés for the same job, a résumé and cover letter now must really stand out. If you have good writing skills and an understanding or experience in human resources, this may be the business right for you. In order to get to know your clients and their experience, talk directly with your clients, rather than just having them electronically fill out a form and send it in to you. Find what unique skills this candidate can offer to employers. Before consulting with the client, have them list what they feel are the top three highlights of their career thus far and why. They also need to give you several accomplishments for each position. If this is their first full-time job, they will list achievements in school, volunteer work, and part-time employment. Consider offering other services, such as job searches, registration, and résumé submission. Also include online articles on your Web site on topics such as the interviewing process, salary negotiation, and performance reviews.

#115   Employment Background Screening

Business overview

Pre-employment screening has become a necessity when hiring employees to avoid lawsuits and costly hiring mistakes. The days are gone when human resources could do an easy reference check and make a few phone calls to screen new employees. Nearly all human resource professionals now use some form of background screening. As a background checker, you will authenticate information given to you by an employer, which could be a business, nonprofit organization, school, or government agency, for a potential job applicant's résumé, application, and/or interviews. Background checking makes the employer confident that the candidate has the skills and experience claimed. Typical background checks include verification of academic credentials and previous employment position, length of service, salary, job performance, and awards. Screenings may trace up to ten years and three previous positions; business, professional, and personal references and letters of recommendation; and criminal background. It is necessary to have knowledge of state and federal regulations for background screening. The federal Fair Credit Reporting Act and state laws put restrictions on applicant and employee background checks and the information that may be used for investigations. You can work with clients through e-mail and phone; you do not need to be in a location near the employer. Rather than being paid per background check, your goal is to contract with companies for a fee to do all their pre-employment investigations. Another option for this business is make additional income by charging advertisers to appear on your site.

Skills needed

Employment background checking firms need to be proficient in the law related to this act, or have a consultant available for this information. Communication and interviewing abilities are essential. Organization and time management are critical to develop necessary programs for the client and set up required forms.

Tips

It is necessary to thoroughly know Internet technology to research information, as well as deliver pre-employment background reports.

Where to find more information

The nonprofit trade association National Association of Professional Background Screeners (**www.napbs.com**) represents organizations that provide employment and background screening.

Sideline Businesses

#116 Online Pre-Employment Personality Assessments

Personality testing of potential employees is a specialty area of background checking you may want to check out. Human resources departments and hiring management need a thorough screening of their employees to know whether a candidate has the skills, ethics, integrity, aptitude, and core competencies to be successful in the position. This reduces employee turnover, increases motivated employees and productivity, and helps to prevent future problems with unethical or criminal behavior. You will offer a series of online assessments for the candidate to complete, and you will analyze them to evaluate whether the candidate should be hired for the position. You will advise the clients on the most effective questionnaire, or test to help them employ the right person. Tests range from simple ten-minute surveys — which provide input on such employment concerns as theft, substance abuse, and anger — to several hour-long tests that look at a candidate's personality and culture. You will need to have experience in human resources, training and development, or psychology for this business. Specialization is also recommended for specific industries, such as education or manufacturing, or for particular functions. There are specific tests, for examples, for accounting, administrative assistants, management potential, sales personnel, and law enforcement.

Chapter 19

Homemade Food

#117 Homemade Food Store

Business overview

Much of the food sold online is homemade and desirable because it is natural and organic. However, it is necessary to be careful regarding regulations. Packaging and shipping also becomes more complex, as does concern for spoilage and product damage. Unless you have previous food distribution experience, you will need to research how to handle, package, and ship food appropriately. You should investigate how the food is regulated on a local, state, and federal level. The Food and Drug Administration (FDA) sets national guidelines, and you can find additional information on their Web site, as well as request written materials. Conduct similar research for on local and state laws regarding the sale of food. A large number of states require a food permit, and the health department will also need to inspect your kitchen. You may need to have a commercial kitchen or a separate kitchen in your home, and you must comply with local license and zoning regulations. Contact your town hall for more information. Insurance coverage is important, especially because you are dealing with food items. Your Web site does not need to be elaborate. Let the food and photographs speak for themselves. You can expand it as your business grows. Buyers need to know how long the product will stay fresh and how and where to store it once it arrives.

Skills needed

This business can be a more difficult Web site to establish than others; it would be helpful if you have had some business experience.

Tips

Conduct considerable research on the safety of your food product, how to safely package and ship the food, and when to discard the food.

Where to find more information

The Natural Products Association (**www.naturalproductsassoc.org**) was established in 1936 and is the country's largest and oldest nonprofit committed to this industry. It has about 10,000 members, including retailers, manufacturers, wholesalers, distributors, supplements, and health and beauty aids.

Sideline Businesses

#118 – 120 Food-Related Web Sites

The following businesses are popular niches for launching for food-related Web sites.

- Tea shop
- Preserves shop
- Pickle shop

#121 Homemade Candy

Business overview

Candy has always been, and always will be, something that people desire. If you are creative and enjoy making sweets, this may be the business for you. Many people are concerned with diet and quality of the product, so you can offer homemade candy with all-natural ingredients. There are so many different types of candy and many different target markets, so your first goal will be to carefully decide on a niche. You should also develop a business plan. Before you begin marketing your candy, check with your local health department to determine what, if any, licensing is needed for a food business. Your house may also need to be inspected by a health department representative to ensure that the location meets requirements. Deciding on the type of candy you will be making is important. Try to offer "free" samples with paid shipping and handling to entice new customers. Purchase the right equipment to make candy in larger batches. You may want to give thought to having customized wrappers in addition to making your own candy. Remember that your packaging is one of your best marketing tools, so be sure to put your name, Web site address, and phone number on the box, if not the wrapper.

Skills needed

Enjoyment and skill for candy making and a good business sense are necessary. This business takes a lot of organization, time management, and marketing abilities.

Tips

If you are going to make the candy at home, it will be necessary to set specific times for working and perhaps a designated "do not touch" area. You do not want to mix business with pleasure.

Where to find more information

The National Confectioners Association (**www.candyusa.com**) promotes the expansion of this industry with the advancement and promotion of its interests and those of consumers.

Sideline Businesses

#122 Fudge Shop

If you enjoy making fudge and have a new marketing idea, this may be a venture to consider. Fudge has long been a much-loved treat and one of the most enjoyable types of candy because of its home-made touch. As with candy making, you are able to work right out of your kitchen. Remember, it is a business, so you will be making many batches of these; making fudge may cease to be enjoyable day in and day out. You may want to consider selling sideline products that go well with fudge. Also, as with candy, look into the need for licensing and health inspections. Your start-up costs will be the cooking equipment and packaging.

#123 Specialized Candy Making

Due to food allergies, the desire for healthy food with natural ingredients, and people who require sugarless candy, you can have a market for specialized candy making for people specific dietary needs. Today, there are many children who cannot have milk or nut products. There are also many people who are allergic to artificial food coloring and other chemical ingredients. Many individuals have low blood sugar or are diabetic. If you enjoy making candy and can tailor your product to these markets, your Web site will be perfect for people who are looking for sweets for themselves or as a gift for others.

Sideline Businesses

#124 Around-the-World Candy

Every country has at least one special type of candy, if not many different kinds. With the world becoming more international, an increasing number of people may want to purchase candy from other nations — even if the taste or texture is different from what they are used to eating. You can buy the candy wholesale or from a drop-ship company and sell it categorized by individual countries, or in a box mixed with different geographical locations around the world.

CASE STUDY: SHERRY COMES

Sherry Comes, President
CoffeeCakes.com
9939 Titan Park Circle
Littleton, CO 80125-9536
1-800-830-2696
www.CoffeeCakes.com

#125 CoffeeCakes.com

One of the best aspects of the Web is the variety of information, services, and products available. The e-commerce and community activities of the millions of online users worldwide truly show how diverse humans are, despite their many similarities. Yahoo! products and services exemplify this diversity, as well.

Who would think, for example, that a Web store specializing in coffee cakes and related gift items would be such a sweet success? (Then again, who can pass up a warm and tasty piece of coffee cake?) President Sherry Comes, who founded **CoffeeCakes.com** in 1995 out of Castle Rock,

Colorado, said, "Since its inception, our Yahoo! store has enjoyed annual growth of about 30 percent." Originally, the company was formed as an Internet coffee shop — the first in Denver — but Comes quickly realized how much better she could do by selling her delicious coffee cakes, and teamed up with Yahoo! to market exclusively online. Now, **CoffeeCakes.com**'s ever-expanding product line includes cheesecakes, whiskey cakes, rum cakes, travel mugs, and more.

When it comes to the Internet and other related electronic communication, Comes knows of what she speaks. As an information technology guru, she was involved with the online world well before most people even knew it was born. Customer service is the No. 1 reason why her company continues to grow. Repeat business is a large portion of sales. A portion of **CoffeeCakes.com**'s profits is donated toward research for Neurofibromatosis (NF) and to help support families affected by the disease. The Yahoo! store's support for this cause was prompted by the fact that Comes' son was diagnosed with the disease in 2005. Gillian Anderson of *The X-Files* is another spokesperson for the NF cause, and the two formed a charitable partnership that supports those affected.

The price of a Yahoo! store is one of the best deals available, according to Comes. What a merchant gets for such a small monthly fee is amazing, especially when considering how well e-commerce sites can do — that is, if the merchant does his or her share of the work. "People have to realize that it is not a 'build it and they shall come,' situation," she said. "Actually, it will be the opposite if a store owner does not invest the necessary time in the business. This is more than a full-time job." A job that has its rewards: Comes received the 2008 "Outstanding Women in Business" award from *The Denver Business Journal* and the National Association of Women Business Owners. With Comes' online store, you can have your cake and eat it, too.

#126 Wedding Cakes

Business overview

According to the Bridal Association of America, the average cost of a wedding cake is $540, and it costs bakeries about 20 percent of this price to make the cake. Each slice can range from $1.50 to $10 depending on how elaborate the cake is. Do people say to you, "Your cakes are so wonderful. Have you ever thought about going into business?" If you are currently making wedding cakes as a hobby, you can now turn this into a lucrative business. Many wedding cake makers have attended a community college or have a bachelor's degree in culinary or baking arts. Consider starting your own "offline" wedding cake business and using the Internet as a means of attracting additional customers in your geographical area. You can use your Web site to display samples of your work and set up appointments. Some wedding cake businesses provide hundreds of different options and allow their customers to design their own special cake. The couple can choose a cake to fit their own particular style in the relaxed atmosphere of their own home. There are also wedding cake Web sites that similarly offer hundreds of pictures of cakes, as well as information about weddings in general. They make money through advertising. You may also consider becoming a wedding salesperson. In this case, you will establish a joint venture with bakeries and caterers, and split the revenue on each cake sold.

Skills needed

Depending on your specific direction in this business, you will need expertise in wedding cake design. Good business and sales skills, and the ability and interest in communicating closely with engaged couples, are necessary.

Tips

Depending on local regulations, you may need a license to bake products in your home for resale purposes. If you are not allowed to start a business at home, check with local bakers about rental arrangements.

Where to find more information

Established in 1918, the Retail Bakers of America (**www.rbanet.com**) is a not-for-profit trade association of about 2,000 retail bakeries and suppliers dedicated to baking industry success.

Sideline Businesses

#127 Special Cake Designs

Special cakes are needed for occasions beyond weddings. These cakes can be used for holidays, birthdays, or other special occasions. The design and shape can be uniquely creative or traditional. You may also want to consider having very elaborately designed cookies to accompany your cake as favors or decorations on the tables. With the latest digital technology, you can easily put a photograph right on the cake or cookies. Edda's Cake Designs (**www.cakedesignsbyedda.com**) offers an example of how you start a successful business designing cakes for occasions other than weddings.

#128 Fortune Cookies

Business overview

If you have an idea for a niche fortune cookie, are clever with words, and like to bake, this may be a business for you. Fortune cookie recipes can be found online or in books. Check with your state health department to find out licensing requirements for selling food out of your home. You may need to have a separate kitchen to make your cookies. Also, look for clever ways to market and package the treats. Fortune cookies can be used as party favors or be sold to traditional Chinese restaurants. Allow customers to write their own notes to go inside the cookie, or design the cookie in a unique shape to carve out your own niche. These can be marketed toward couples planning a wedding or anyone planning a party for multiple occasions. Use all the marketing tools available, including online social net-works and SEO. You may also want to send out a sample to anyone who shows serious interest in your product.

Skills needed

Baking skills are a must. You must be creative enough to come up with a new niche in this saturated industry.

Tips

Be sure to line up extra help for busier times. Keeping to a schedule and get-ting the orders out on time is imperative. Carefully follow the regulations for noting ingredients for your cookies. If your products are made around certain ingredients, such as nuts, you will need to notify customers.

Where to find more information

Fancy Fortune Cookies (**www.fancyfortunecookies.com**) is a great exam-ple of how to create a business selling personalized fortune cookies.

Sideline Businesses

#129 Ethnic or Holiday Cookies

Do you have a special cookie you traditionally make for a religious or ethnic holiday or celebration that others may find enjoyable? What about a special type of gingerbread man, hamantashen, amaretti, medianyky, pfeffernüesse, fattigmann, bizcochitos, kolachie, chocolate Florentine, spumoni, or Chinese almond? Construct a Web site that high-lights the holiday or celebration and the history of the cookie. Offer sug-gestions on how customers can start a new tradition involving the treats.

Chapter 20

Going Green

#130 Green Businesses

Business overview

A variety of businesses are popping up online with a general "green" theme. Depending on your interest, skills, and available funds, there are many businesses to start. Or, you can come up with a completely unique green business. One option is to recycle old objects to be used for another item. For example, you may want to collect and sell old costume jewelry that can be made into other pieces. Or, use the recycled goods to develop your own green craft. Many people with a "green thumb" are coming up with ideas such as paper beads; quilts, backpacks, and purses from recycled materials; or recycling T-shirts into stylish children's clothes. Research ways in which products and foods were made in the past without additives and chemicals. Can you start a business selling food using green techniques? Are you crafty? What about making green products for babies, such as bedding, clothing, diapers, and lotions? Or, give thought to making green lotions, skin care, and cosmetics for men and women, such as soaps, insect repellents, massage lotions, and make up. Do not forget about e-books. Many people are interested in knowing how to become more environmentally friendly. Also, consider developing a green directory with a list of green businesses. Many consumers are looking to only shop with businesses using green technology.

Skills needed

You should be knowledgeable on the latest green trends to know what will be a hit in this industry.

Tips

Look at green directories, such as **http://onlinegreendirectory.com**, to see which niches are already saturated.

Where to find more information

The Green Business Association (**www.greenbusinesses.net**) consists of companies working toward saving the environment.

Sideline Businesses

#131   Green Gift Giving

Instead of making your own products, have other businesses market their green products through you. You can have an entire site devoted to green gifts customized for each holiday, such as flower seeds for Mother's Day and recycled paper cards for Valentine's Day. You will either charge the businesses upfront for selling on your Web site, or take a commission on each item sold. Before including an item, get a sample. You want all your products to be of the highest quality. Also, since these businesses will be packaging and sending out their items, you need to make sure the products are shipped within 24 hours of ordering. You do not want to lose your credibility over another business's customer service problems.

Sideline Businesses

#132 Herbs

Herbs have been used for drinks and medicinal purposes for thousands of years. According to the American Botanical Council, herbal dietary supplement sales in the United States increased slightly in 2008, reaching a total estimated figure of $4.8 million. They are used for decorations, cosmetics, medicine, aromatics, and foods. If you are growing herbs for a hobby, perhaps you want to spice up your income with this business. The popularity of herbs offers an opportunity for herb gardeners everywhere to develop a successful business growing and selling these fresh-cut herbs. Herbs are in large demand because of the increased interest in culinary delights, as well as natural health care treatments. They are used for home remedies and cooking, as well as for herbal balms, oils, and ointments when dried. The more information you have on your site about the plants, recipes, medical uses, and other similar articles, the easier it will be to sell your products. You can sell the herbs by seeds, pots, or plug trays. In addition to culinary herbs, you may also want to sell related products, such as loose herbal tea and aromatics. Always be sure to note to customers that the information you provide is for educational purposes only.

Chapter 21

Health Care

#133 Medical Transcription Services

Business overview

Medical care is becoming increasingly complicated and litigation more common. It comes as no surprise that the medical transcription business is increasing significantly, as well. It is necessary to transcribe copies of dictated notes related to physicals and diagnostic procedures in order to document patient histories, legal evidence for patient care, and facts on which diagnosis and treatments were made. Insurance companies may also want transcriptions before paying doctors. It is quite easy to start a medical transcription business: Start-up costs are low, and you only need basic equipment, including a transcription machine, cassette player, and reference books. You will need to buy some software, such as a medical spell-checker and a word expander utility that converts abbreviations and reduces the amount of actual typing. Microsoft Word actually includes this utility. It is not necessary to have a degree in medical transcription to start your business, but you may want to take a medical transcription course at the local community college or through adult education to get the basics. Medical transcription is usually paid by the amount of work completed.

Therefore, it is quite normal to charge your clients by the line, or at an hourly rate.

Skills needed

This is a business that requires training or experience before you are able to start your own business.

Tips

There are a number of different sites online for finding freelance medical transcription work.

Where to find more information

The Association for Healthcare Documentation Integrity (**www.ahdionline. org**) is committed to advancing health care capture and documentation.

#134 Medical Billing and Coding Services

Business overview

A doctor's livelihood depends on billing patients and receiving payment on a timely basis. Although the health care industry continues to grow significantly, it is also becoming more complex. Private and government-administered insurance companies, HMOs, PPOs, and many other types of plans have made billing very complicated. Although some physicians have established internal billing departments, many hire external medical billing services for such services as invoicing, collecting co-payments, tracking uncollectibles, and responding to inquiries. By acting as a one-person accounts-receivable department, you will help your clients apply health care coding, bill patients, and process, and send doctor's claims to insurance companies. In addition, you will track down unpaid claims and brief doctors on patient numbers. The way to be successful in this business is to obtain a strong and trusting relationship with your clients. Medical billers differ on the services they offer. Some take charge of all responsibilities, handling everything involved with the office's accounting needs — from submitting electronic claims for insurance and billing patients, to tracking account payables and receivables. Others specialize by only handling insurance claim submissions. To be paid for their services, most medical billing and coding services take a percentage of what the health care providers charge on each transaction or charge on an hourly basis.

Skills needed

You should not go into the medical billing field without some experience or training in the field. If you have not previously worked for a doctor, dentist, or alternative health care provider, you will want to take a course in coding and billing at your local community college.

You will need to learn basics about medical terminology, the insurance claim life cycle, insurance forms, and the procedures of each of the different insurance companies for medical insurance and third-party reimbursements.

Tips

In addition to your standard rates, you may want to charge clients an initial processing fee to obtain all the details about their insurance companies and claim structure.

Beware of scams that offer medical billing training. Make sure the institution you decide to attend is accredited.

Where to find more information

The American Health Information Management Association (**www. ahima.org**) offers educational resources and programs to medical records professionals.

Sideline Businesses

#135   Medical Claims Assistance Professional

Many patients, especially those who have been chronically ill or had a major illness, injury, or surgery, need assistant with being reimbursed for their medical claims. In many cases, these are older individuals who do not have the ability to fill out forms, make call after call, or fight against red tape, especially if they are still not feeling great. Physicians must file Medicare claims for their patients, but have the flexibility on how to secure reimbursement from private insurance carriers. Patients, who may need to be quickly reimbursed because of their lower income, appreciate someone else who understands their dilemma and can talk directly to the insurance companies and determine the status of the claim. To be a claims assistance professional (CAP), you need a thorough understanding of the insurance claim processing system and be able to spend a great deal of your time on the phone contacting physicians and insurance carriers. You will work directly with the patients who need to be reimbursed for their medical claims. You will make sure bills are accurate, provide patients with their options, and decipher and manage paperwork for the client. If the patient is uninsured, you will help negotiate provider costs and make sure there are no unforeseen charges. You will work with both insurance companies and physicians to determine how fees can be lowered and decisions disputed. You will also assist in selecting Medicare plans, making choices during open enrollment periods, providing education on benefits and options, and negotiating providers' fees for uninsured patients or procedures. Because this is an online business, you will first talk with patients over the phone about their specific needs, assess the situation, and provide them with an idea of how much it will cost to resolve the issue. You may want to offer the first hour for free. For more information, visit **www.claims.org**.

#136   Home Companions

Business overview

When a person gets older, they may have trouble attending to household duties, such as cooking or cleaning. Help may also be needed to run errands or help seniors attend events. Many times, when a spouse has passed away or lives in a health care facility, the husband or wife left at home needs someone to talk to. A home companion is not responsible for health care, bathing, or dressing. They may often make sure the proper medicine has been taken and in the right dosage or a recommended diet is being followed, but time is usually spent being a helping hand. Some tasks include cooking, laundry, lifting heavy objects, driving, and shopping. You can start a business matching home companions with those in need of this service. Both the companions and family members register and create a profile about themselves and the services required. You can offer links to providers or affiliates, offering background checks on your Web site where you will be paid a commission when their services are used. You may also choose to provide a background check as part of or as an added service to the home companion's fee.

Skills needed

You should be patient and compassionate. It is a good idea to have basic cooking and cleaning skills.

Tips

Make it very clear to customers that this is not a health care or home health aide position. The family member should not ask the home companion to do any health care or personal hygiene work.

Also stress that background checks be completed before a home companion is hired, and that you are not responsible for those who register on the site. Home companions should also be advised to talk with the family member and meet the person needing care before making a final decision on whether to take the position.

Where to find more information

Home Companion Services (**http://homecompanion.com**) is an excellent resource for starting your business.

#137 Geriatric Consultant

Business overview

As the population ages and many children need to make decisions regarding their aging parents, many are turning to geriatric consultants to help them handle the transition. These consultants provide valuable information and advocacy for family members. If you have a background or experience in elder care and enjoy working closely with people, this would be an excellent opportunity. Because this is an online business, you will not meet personally with the clients, but rather will market yourself as an expert who can answer questions and conduct research. For example, you can find what assisted living locations are in a certain area of the country, or provide alternatives to nursing homes. You may also be asked to answer questions regarding Medicare and Medicaid coverage. If you already have previous experience in gerontology, health care, social work, or a related field, starting this type of business will be an easy transition. It is necessary to thoroughly understand Medicare, Medicaid, and long-term insurance, as well as financial issues concerning the elderly. If a family wants to meet personally with a consultant for an assessment of their parent's health, home, and present/future living situation, you can find a licensed geriatric care professional through the National Association of Professional Geriatric Care Managers.

Skills needed

It is important to have a background in elder care, and the ability to respond to all types of questions concerning geriatric issues.

Tips

You will charge per hour for your phone consultation and research if required.

Where to find more information

The National Association of Professional Geriatric Care Managers (**www. caremanager.org**) is trade organization of professionals involved in geriatric care.

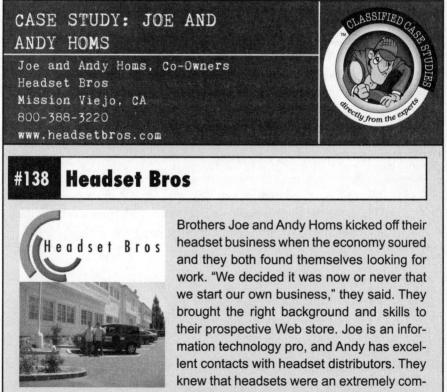

CASE STUDY: JOE AND
ANDY HOMS

Joe and Andy Homs, Co-Owners
Headset Bros
Mission Viejo, CA
800-388-3220
www.headsetbros.com

CLASSIFIED CASE STUDIES
directly from the experts

#138 Headset Bros

Headset Bros

Brothers Joe and Andy Homs kicked off their headset business when the economy soured and they both found themselves looking for work. "We decided it was now or never that we start our own business," they said. They brought the right background and skills to their prospective Web store. Joe is an information technology pro, and Andy has excellent contacts with headset distributors. They knew that headsets were an extremely competitive and saturated market. Yet, they also knew they had an advantage over most of these many other merchants — strong customer service.

"Our relationship with suppliers lets us offer products at a lower price and give our customers quick, free shipping," Joe said. He explains that drop-ship companies do not have one set price for their services. What they charge depends on a variety of factors, including their association with their customers. Forming these bonds with suppliers helps the Homs brothers acquire other reputable distributors, because they are "constantly looking for new products." Joe said that it is beneficial to talk with many distributors at a time and "pit one against the other in terms of cost." Naturally, a good price must also go hand-in-hand with their customer service reputation. To ensure that his drop-ship companies are meeting the Headset Bros' needs, Andy regularly uses an alias "to drop ship something to myself" to make sure the products are shipped, packaged, correct, and up to his standards. There is nothing that discourages repeat sales more than an order not in stock, a wrong product shipped out, or an item packaged incorrectly.

As with other growing Web stores, Joe and Andy spend a great deal of time marketing their products and site. They primarily use organic marketing, such as search engine keywords, link exchanges, and social networking. They have used some Google AdWords and established affiliate marketing relationships. They find that specials, such as giving away a free item along with a purchase, helps "sell products like hot cakes." Also, a listing on such sites as **www.pricegrabber.com**, which compares products and merchant deals, as well as eBay and Amazon, also boosts traffic. "We're always experimenting on ways to get our name out to the public. We are constantly measuring every part of our business and making things better," said Joe. With so many vying for the same customers, "we need to differentiate ourselves and let potential customers know that we can provide service unlike anyone else."

Chapter 22
Internet

#139 Electronic Magazine Publishing

Business overview

An online magazine is a Web-based site targeting a niche or specialized subject area and population of readers. Some of these magazines focus on business, and others are written directly for a consumer market. Similar to traditional print magazines, these online publications blend news, editorials, feature stories, and reviews. Actually, you can see your magazine as a well-developed blog: Instead of just offering your own views on a specific subject, you are also incorporating the articles of professionals in your specific field of interest. The online magazine publishing industry is doing quite well. It is much less expensive to publish online and, with easy-to-use blogging or Web site packages, designing an e-zine is simple. Income can be generated through traditional selling of ad space, links to affiliate Web sites selling product or services related to your niche, and Google AdSense. The key to online magazine publishing is deciding on the topic. You must find a niche of interest to a large population, but one that is not already being filled. Plan the type of articles you will have, the intended authors, the thematic slant, and the primary purpose for the publication. Define your means of income generation.

Skills needed

Because it is necessary to wear all hats — publisher, salesperson, editor-in-chief, author, article acquisition editor, and designer — this takes a well-rounded entrepreneur.

Tips

This is a perfect business for a writer/editor who has a keen business sense.

Where to find more information

Magazine Launch (**www.magazinelaunch.com**) connects vendors and consultants with publishing professionals and entrepreneurs starting consumer, trade, special interest, and organizational magazines.

CASE STUDY:
STEPHEN WINDWALKER

Stephen Windwalker (pen name)
Harvard Perspectives Press
Cambridge, MA
http://indiekindle.blogspot.com

#140 Harvard Perspectives Press

In addition to publishing other authors' works through his own company Harvard Perspectives Press, Stephen Windwalker started writing and publishing his own books and marketing them through Amazon and his own Web site. He began with *Selling Used Books Online* in 2002, because of his past experience as a bookseller.

When Amazon introduced its Kindle electronic reader, Windwalker was an immediate fan. As an Amazon affiliate, he began selling Kindles, and in 2008 published another book, *Beyond the Literary-Industrial Complex: How Authors and Publishers Are Using the Amazon Kindle and Other*

New Technologies to Unleash a 21st-Century Indie Movement of Readers & Writers. From the start, Windwalker saw the Kindle as a perfect vehicle for emerging, independent, and self-published authors to beta-test or introduce their books — either in completed form or as excerpts. He also introduced another blog/Web site specifically devoted to promoting the Kindle.

While completing his own book on Kindle, he excerpted chapters as freestanding articles for Kindle readers. His readership quickly mounted to the Kindle bestseller list. He had more than 1,400 readers in the first few weeks and, a few months later, sold 20,000 "copies" of his work. Not thinking that his downloads would rise this fast, Windwalker promised his 10-year-old son his own Kindle once they had 8,000 downloads. Needless to say, his son now has his own Kindle.

Windwalker understands how to take advantage of online marketing opportunities. He has two blogs that promote the Kindle, is an Amazon affiliate, and sells his own books through Amazon. He says Amazon has a very strong search infrastructure that has helped promote his sites.

He emphasizes that anyone who wants to sell a book to be read on a Kindle can do that now, by promoting the content as a text file download, or by selling it as a text file on a CD. In addition, there is a great deal of free literary content available through Kindle.

#141 Search Engine Optimization Service

Business overview

Research finds that more than 85 percent of Internet users locate new Web sites by using the primary search engines. Similarly, other studies conclude that search engine searching is one of the most popular activities on the Web and a critical part of a business' online marketing strategy. It is now clearly recognized that Web site ranking on the first or second page of Google or one of the other major search engines or social networks can lead to huge increases in sales and high-quality traffic. Search Engine Optimization (SEO) is becoming increasingly sophisticated and now includes consulting, keyword recommendations, copywriting, Web site redevelopment, link formation, search engine submission, and SEO result reports. As an SEO specialist, you will consult with your client on the best ways to optimize a Web site. Along with a variety of SEO strategies, you will provide additional help with other areas of marketing, such as blogs, e-mails, and social networking. Companies may hire your SEO business for several different reasons: 1) to help build high-quality content for attracting search engines and visitors; 2) to make the Web site work better as an affiliate marketing partner; and 3) to have a means for increased revenue.

Skills needed

An advanced knowledge of the Internet, search engine marketing, and optimization is necessary.

Tips

In addition to having a strong understanding and experience in the Internet and marketing, you need to be well-versed in online technology and Google Analytics. It is necessary for you to analyze the SEO additions made on the client's Web site to determine the impact on overall marketing efforts.

Another option for this business is make additional income by charging advertisers to appear on your site.

Where to find more information

SEOTutorial (**www.SEOtutorial.info**) is a good source of basic information for SEO.

#142 Virtual Tours

Business overview

Traditionally, travelers have plotted vacations through countries with the use of travel books. Now, travelers can use virtual tours with video to learn about a specific city, town, village, or countryside. If viewing these before their trip, they can make informed decisions on where to visit and carefully plot out daily activities. If they wait to view the videos online from their hotel or an Internet café, they can grab a local map and plot out each day's new adventure. Videos are free for the visitors, but you charge advertisers to list rentals, recreation activities, hotels, and restaurants. In addition, you may offer videos of special events, such as Colonial Williamsburg, Virginia, along with local advertisements. With the videos, you will provide a map featuring advertiser's locations. You also need to provide a background on the history, geography, political situation, food, culture, and weather of the location, as well as traveling tips, time zones, traveler warnings, health information, and newsgroups for more information. Another option for this business is make additional income by charging advertisers to appear on your site. Many sites make an income in this manner, as advertisers will pay to advertise on a site that attracts a large number of customers. Market to advertisers that relate to the area of business you are covering.

Skills needed

It helps if you have a great deal of travel experience, or if you are familiar with world geography. An advanced knowledge of the Internet is also important.

Tips

You can expand your videos by making arrangements with other locations, such as museums, universities, and realtors. You can gradually increase information about your various tourist locations with music. Ask people to send in their photographs and tips about their travels.

Where to find more information

Virtual Tourist (**www.virtualtourist.com**) is an excellent example of this type of business. Visit this site to get ideas for your business.

CASE STUDY: CHRIS MALTA

Chris Malta, Founder/CEO
Worldwide Brands, Inc.
2250 Lucien Way, STE 250
Maitland, Florida 32751
www.worldwidebrands.com

#143 Worldwide Brands, Inc.

After spending several years as a Microsoft-certified systems engineer designing and building corporate and e-commerce networks, Chris Malta started looking for products to sell online. He quickly discovered that the search engines were full of scammers and "junk" directories, not genuine wholesalers. "Through trial-and-error, I developed a process for locating and qualifying legitimate wholesalers who would work with online sellers like myself. To make a long story short, I realized many online sellers needed help finding reliable product sources, and **WorldwideBrands.com** was born," Malta said.

"We publish the Internet's largest directory of fully verified wholesalers and drop shippers willing to work with online retailers. You get instant access to thousands of wholesalers, representing millions of quality products for stocking Web stores, with a built-in market research tool to help identify profitable product markets," he said. The site also offers a full-time research staff dedicated to qualifying new suppliers based on the merchant's requests. The seller saves months of tedious, time-consuming research and trial-and-error learning.

But Worldwide Brands is not only for experienced vendors. The solutions are simple and user-friendly for new e-commerce people, and the Web site offers a significant amount of free education to help new online sellers start the business in the right direction. "Our sellers range from brand-new start-ups to well-established retailers who sell millions each year," said Malta. Shawna Fennell, owner of **1Choice4YourStore. com,** said, "Chris has helped so many people. I wouldn't be here today without [his] services."

Malta offers a tip to those who are ready to order products for their business: "When you're selling online, the most important thing is to know that you're working with factory-authorized wholesalers. Whether you find them on your own or through a trusted resource like **WorldwideB-rands.com**, working directly with real wholesale suppliers and getting real wholesale prices allows your business to be competitive in the online market and achieve the highest possible profits every time." The suppliers registered at Worldwide have all been contacted and provided their contact information, order requirements, and Web site URL. "We've talked to each of these suppliers. They're *expecting* to hear from online sellers and are ready to work with them," he said.

As of this writing, Malta is traveling throughout the United States with his own special cause: warning people to beware of Internet scams promising you can make millions overnight, just by handing over money for a Web site and product, going to sleep, and seeing the money in your PayPal account the next morning. But the same holds true online as is does in the real world: If it sounds too good, it is too good.

#144 Screensavers

Business overview

Screensavers may not be a new concept, but that does not mean they are not still in demand. According to Yahoo!, the term "screensaver" has been a top search word since 1995. Search engine word trackers report that the word "screensaver" continues to be searched at least 30,000 times daily. With today's advanced technology and your computer knowhow, you can create screensavers that are unique and trendy. You can market customized screensavers to both businesses and individuals. People are looking for one-of-a-kind products that define themselves. These screensavers can capture the faces of families and friends, vacation pleasures, memorable times, and events and holidays. They can also be given as gifts and favors at reunions and special occasions. Screen savers can be made from any-one's photographs, video, or Flash animation with the addition of sound and music. Companies can use the screen savers in their branding strategy and promotion, incorporating their logo, products, and taglines, and passing the free product out to present and potential customers. If you are creating a Web site offering generic screensavers, customers will likely not want to pay for your creations, as many screensavers can be found for free on their own computers and from other free sites on the Internet. If this is the case, you will need to make an income by charging advertisers to show ads on your site.

Skills needed

An advanced knowledge of using design software is imperative.

Tips

Develop screensavers that are of interest to niche markets, such as vegetarians, joggers, moviegoers, antique collectors, or mountain climbers. Promote the advantages of your screensavers over "free" products, which are often spyware and illegitimate. Offer free screensavers to customers and make an income by charging advertisers to market their products or services on your Web site.

Where to find more information

Screensaver.com (**www.screensaver.com**) is an excellent example of this type of business. Visit this site for ideas on building your business.

Chapter 23

Service Businesses

#145 Private Investigator

Business overview

Do you have strong research skills and the ability to find information? Have you ever solved problems in your personal life by getting all the facts? Do you have experience in law? The U.S. Bureau of Labor forecasts that the demand for private investigators will increase 25 percent by 2012. As a private investigator, your business will involve working with the public, not the government or police. You will be involved with areas of fraud, infidelity, and extortion. You may also help people find unclaimed funds, conduct background checks for employers and apartment owners, handle trademark searches, and assist with adoption reunions. Most successful private investigators specialize and establish their expertise in one or two related areas. For example, they may specialize in computer crime, employee background investigations, or insurance fraud. Your area will depend on previous work experience. It is important that your Web site is professional and specifically explains the services you offer.

Skills needed

You may need to take a course to fine-tune your skills. Depending on state requirements, some private investigators must pass a written examination on laws and regulations. Licensing for private investigators varies from state to state. Be sure to carefully investigate the course, as there are many scams in this area. You should also consider becoming certified by the National Association of Legal Investigators.

Tips

Keep up-to-date on changes in the industry. Forensics is continually being updated, and it may significantly impact your business.

There are many unqualified private investigators who are listed with the Better Business Bureau as not properly performing their services. Follow the licensing requirements and the private investigators code of ethics. Always have references to show potential clients.

Where to find more information

The Private Investigators Association of America (**http://privateinvestigatorsassociation.com**) is a nonprofit association for providing an educational forum for investigators to enhance the skills and the level of professionalism of industry members.

#146 Gift Baskets

Business overview

When someone wants a unique present for a friend, business associate, or family member, customers enjoy the convenience of shopping for gift baskets online. These baskets can be tailored to fit the recipient's interests. The business puts together a unique, one-of-a-kind basket for the recipient. Creating a niche is an important part of this business. In order to be successful, you should specialize in gift baskets for specific events, such as wedding showers, romantic picnics, baby arrivals, graduation gifts, or work promotions. You can go as far as your creativity will let you. Some gift basket businesses, for example, are combining the benefits of two ventures in one: gift baskets and private label food. The baskets contain gourmet delicacies and snacks labeled with the gift business's name and logo. Gift baskets make perfect gifts for employees, customers, and vendors, thus corporate settings and businesses may provide substantial business. One of the biggest advantages is that this business can be started with just a few hundred dollars.

Skills needed

This business requires preparation, commitment, and a great deal of time and enthusiasm to provide the gift of gifting.

Tips

To keep your costs low when you first start your business, do not buy a lot of products from online wholesale companies. First, understand the demand for specific products; otherwise, you may end up with a hundred bottles of hot peppers. Pick up clearance items that can be used in a variety of different baskets.

Where to find more information

Design It Yourself Gifts and Baskets (**www.designityourselfgiftbaskets. com**) is an excellent example of this type of business. Visit this site to brainstorm ideas for your business.

#147 Genealogy Service

Business overview

Increasing numbers of people are searching for their family roots and creating family trees. This is a painstaking process that often takes a great deal of research and knowledge of how to access genealogical information. Some customers will do as much as they can to fill in the tree, but then will turn to expert specialists to track down the more difficult aspects of their history. Or, there are some people who want to tackle this project on their own and need a consultant to get them started. In this business, you will talk with interested customers about the services they require and charge customers per hour or per specific projects/research. You will either give instructions on how they can conduct the research, or actually find the information yourself. You will spend a great deal of time online, reading e-mails, and possibly researching on location. It will be necessary for you to establish contacts through organizations that can help you get specific information. Join genealogical societies and continually improve your research and writing skills, comparing your abilities to other genealogists.

Skills needed

Excellent research skills are required in this business.

Tips

People love to talk and tell others all about their family. You are charging by the hour, so be very careful of your time. Create a specific set of questions or a survey to stay on-topic.

Also offer space on your Web site for potential paid advertisements, which are always an option for extra income.

Where to find more information

The National Association of Professional Genealogists (**www.ap-gen.org**) promotes learning, services, and ethical standards of its members.

CASE STUDY:
ABBY SCHMELLING

Abby Schmelling
Genealogy Photo Detective
708-366-7396
http://genealogyphotodetective.com

#148 Genealogy Photo Detective

 Genealogy is becoming increasingly popular, as people search to find their ancestral roots and create their family trees. There are numerous Web sites that offer to help individuals track down their ancestors or draw their family trees. Abby Schmelling, who has long been interested in genealogy and attends and speaks at genealogical conferences, decided she should go another route online to be able to distinguish herself from all these other specialists. Because photography is another one of her interests, and many people are looking for photographs to accompany their ancestral memoirs, Schmelling realized that being a genealogical photo detective would be a perfect niche.

Niches are an advantage because they separate the Web site entrepreneur from the competitors. However, it can also be a challenge when the niche is relatively new and people do not know these services exist. This presents another important reason for marketing: Getting the word out that you can help families and organizations in their research, even if they do not know you can. "I'm finding that search engine optimization, having the right keywords, is really a big plus in my marketing," said Schmelling. When users search for words such as genealogy, historical photos, surnames, genealogy research, genealogy history, grave pictures, and historical cemetery, Schmelling's Web site comes up. Because the site is only several months old, she will push social networking and links with common Web sites. Plus, she needs to write more articles and copy to draw interest from search engines and interested individuals. "When you have a niche of a niche like I have," Schmelling said, "you have to learn the best way to reach everyone who needs and wants your services." Since she is a detective, she will surely find the right answers.

#149 House Sitting Service

Business overview

People often spend a lot of time away from their homes. They go away on quick business trips, weekends for fast getaways, and vacations throughout the year. When they leave, their pets, plants, and home's safety are a concern. Hiring a house sitter can be very advantageous. This is a business that does not need a lot of overhead, but you will need an understanding of how to design a Web site. Your Web site fills the need of both the sitter and the homeowner. Income can be generated in a number of different ways. One common approach is to charge to list the house sitters. They can pay a quarterly or yearly charge. The people who need a house sitter typically do not pay for your service. Another option for this business is make additional income by charging advertisers to appear on your site. Market to advertisers that relate to the area of business you are covering.

You will not screen house sitters who register on your site, but you should encourage homeowners to do so. You can also team up with businesses that conduct background checks and offer a discount on this service.

Skills needed

You should have an excellent command of navigating the Internet and working with advertisers to bring in extra income.

Tips

Become a member of the biggest social networks, such as MySpace, to get the word out about your services, as well as exchange links with other sites and blogs and join forums. Promote other benefits for this service. For instance, for the owners, it is the security of having someone is their house. For the house sitter, it is having a place to stay when visiting another part of the country or world. Make sure homeowners know you have not screened the house sitters registered on your site; it is up to them to conduct a background check on any possible sitters and talk with them to establish a degree of comfort.

Where to find more information

House Sitters America (**http://housesittersamerica.com**) is an excellent example of how you can start a business in this industry.

#150 Selling Used Car Parts

Business overview

Many car parts can be repaired and reused, and used car parts are much more affordable than buying new parts. As a result, a large number of people are searching online to find specific parts, and a growing amount of Web sites offer these parts for extra income. They scour flea markets and salvage yards to find discarded parts. If you are knowledgeable in mechanics, enjoy fixing cars, and can tell a potentially profitable used part when you see one, you may want to get into the business. You will spend a great deal of time in junkyards and at used car part recyclers, who will usually quote a very reasonable price for the resale of a part.

There are also used part wholesalers who will sell you parts in bulk. A section of your Web site should list any vintage car parts you have for sale. The price for this category of part will be much higher than the others you are selling. Make sure that you advertise these parts because they are difficult to find, and customers searching for a specific part will definitely be interested. For extra income, set up a classified section on your Web site and allow customers run an ad requesting a certain part. Also consider paid advertisements to be run on your site.

Skills needed

An understanding of automotive technology is critical.

Tips

Instead of selling antique parts individually, collect a set of them and hold an auction. If you know someone is looking for a specific part, buy it from another used-part seller like yourself. As long as you get a good mark-up on the item, it does matter where you find it. You need to know a good part from a damaged one, and be very clear to the customers that an item is sold "as is."

Where to find more information

GetUsedParts.com (**www.getusedparts.com**) is an example of how you can turn your automobile knowledge into a thriving business.

CASE STUDY: CHIP BULKELEY

Chip Bulkeley, Owner
CHiP's V6 Specialties
Fort Worth, Texas
817-726-2781
www.chipsv6specialties.com

CLASSIFIED CASE STUDIES
directly from the experts

#151 CHiP's V6 Specialties

Chip Bulkeley, owner of CHiPs V6 Specialties, has used the power of Yahoo! Merchant Solutions to increase the sales power of his business. In 2003, Chip and Linda Bulkeley were spending "tons of time" searching the Internet for information on how to fix up their 1997-3.8L V6 Ford Mustang. His father wisely asked, "Did you ever think about setting up your own Web site for Mustang V6 and GT enthusiasts?" After initially thinking, "You've got to be kidding," Bulkeley saw the wisdom in this question. "We wanted a site that would cater to the beginner and beyond."

He started looking around for a way to start his new Web site and balked at the prices of $10,000 to $15,000 quoted by designers. Then, he read about Yahoo! and decided the $39.95 monthly Internet service provider fee to build the site was much easier to digest. With the help of the 384-page *Web-site Getting Started* guide and the 24/7 customer service team, "little by little," he said, "I grew my site. There never was a time when someone in customer service didn't help me."

In 2006, at the request of his visitors, he began adding V6 Mustang performance products and upgrade kits to his Web site. He now has agreements with five wholesalers and still finds it quite easy to add and change his product listings. He is pleased to see that Yahoo! is improving its search functions with the Store Manager function, which has been a problem in the past. Also, when Yahoo! signed an agreement with Pay-Pal for the shopping cart, Bulkeley's sales went up 35 percent.

Bulkeley is glad he went with Yahoo! to develop his online business, not only because of the price and ease of use, but also because of the brand name. He knows the Yahoo! Secure Buyer Protection statement on his site shows that he is a reputable merchant. He also knows Yahoo! keeps its quality levels high: "If you prove yourself less than above-board, Yahoo! kicks you out," he said. Anyone who understands the high quality and performance of the Mustang V6 knows that the Web site must convey that same quality.

Chapter 24

Photography

Do you enjoy taking photographs? You may want to consider starting a photography business, offering your services through your Web site as well as on-site. Because of the expense, you will need to already have most of your photographic equipment to stay within the $1,000 budget. Many of these areas require extensive knowledge of photography and skills specific to the niche. Commercial clients may contact you through your Web site to take artistic or promotional photographs for print or online magazines, newsletters, or newspapers. Or, you may get a call or e-mail from someone wanting a photograph for personal reasons. The following photography business niches only skim the service of this broad industry.

#152 Weddings

Today, wedding photographers need to be more creative than ever, with the wide variety of weddings being performed in various settings. Still, digital technology has greatly enhanced photography and, in many respects, made the career easier. You should be prepared to take traditional wedding portraits and more creative photos, as well. You will conduct business outside and indoors at a variety of location. Along with photographing the ceremony and reception, you can also offer engagement photos and bridal portraits.

#153 Portraits

Portrait photographers not only need the technical and artistic skills, but also strong communication skills to relax the people being photographed and bring their personality into the photo. If you are doing studio shots, you will need room in your home or office, or you will need to rent studio space. You can specialize in an area, such as children or pets, or photography in indoor or outdoor locations. Photos can also be taken with the subjects posed or in action.

#154 Sporting Events

Schools, community organizations, or professional teams are often looking for photographers who can take pictures of private and public school and community-wide sporting events. With digital cameras, you can automatically determine whether you have the right shot or need to catch a similar scene. You will be taking both action shots of the games, as well as team and individual photographs.

#155 School Activities

In addition to sports, there are many other activities taking place in public school or university settings where a photographer is needed. These photos are used for both print and online communication. Yearbook publishing companies often need help as well, especially at special times of the year when all the students need their photos taken.

#156 Aerial Photography

Aerial photography is taken from an airplane, helicopter, or balloon. Photos can be used for press purposes, publishing, real estate, law firms, historical information, and research purposes; or, they can simply be beautiful photos used for decoration.

#157 Architectural or Real Estate

Architectural photography includes views of the exterior and interior of domestic, commercial, religious, institutional, and engineering structures, in addition to recording the development of towns and cities. You may travel anywhere around the world to get these shots.

#158 Documentary

Photojournalism is the art of telling a story, whether news- or feature-related, through photos. It is a special talent and requires knowing how to capture an important story in one quick shot. Your photographs may appear in newspapers on- and offline, as well as in books. Photojournalists often travel to different cities and countries to get their pictures. Your Web site will help promote your services worldwide.

#159 Forensic

The photographer supports the forensic scientist, toxicologist, and medical examiner by documenting evidence, crime scenes, and autopsies. The photographer also takes pictures for displays and graphics for court proceedings, training, and Web sites.

#160 Nature

Photographs of nature are enjoyed by everyone. They can be used as pieces of art or for educational purposes. You may also travel around the world to get your photos, and a Web site will help in your marketing efforts. You may also want to specialize in a specific type of nature.

#161 Panoramic

Many organizations want 360-degree photographs of buildings or geographical locations. These photos are also appreciated for their natural, artistic style.

#162 Travel

If you enjoy traveling from one location to another, then this type of photography may be for you. Although the competition is plentiful, you can specialize in a certain part of the world, or be on-call whenever a photographer is needed.

#163 Astrophotography

This niche centers on using a telescope to take and sell photographs of space for artistic purposes. You can offer many different types of astronomical images, like noctilucent clouds, aurora borealis, the moon, the sun, and beautiful scenery shots.

Sideline Businesses

#164 Stock Photography

It can be lucrative to start your own stock photography service in a niche area because many businesses do not have the time to hire their own photographers or they may need a photo at the last minute. Stock photography is equivalent to a library of photographs, allowing a client to purchase pictures for one-time use. It is imperative, however, that the photographs be of excellent quality, exposure, resolution, and composition, due to the competitive nature of this art. By conducting a search for the various stock photography Web sites, you will be able to view the best and the worst of what is available.

#165 Tintype Photographs

Many people are nostalgic for the "good old days." They may like digital photographs, but also enjoy collecting old photographs, including tintypes, which were the first photographs ever printed. You can use an inkjet printer and aluminum sheets to make your own tintypes from digital photos. These aluminum tintype sheets can be used with any inkjet systems, including dye- and pigment-based inks. The ink you use will determine the printed image's longevity. It is best to use archival grade inks for long-term durability if prolonged ultraviolet exposure occurs.

#166 Photo Transfer Service

You can offer the transfer of photographs on a multitude of objects, such as ceramic cups, porcelain plaques, ceramic tiles, canvas, material, or even edible paper for cakes and candy. One of the more interesting uses of photography is a photographic quilt to honor a graduate, remember a loved one, or commemorate a special occasion. This is also a service that can be added to any other photography business to earn extra income.

Chapter 25

Special Events

#167 Diaper Cake Businesses

Business overview

Baby showers are just as popular today as they have been in past decades. Diaper cakes are a new trend at baby showers that is a perfect business for a creative entrepreneur. A diaper cake is a collection of diapers rolled and stacked together to resemble a traditional tiered wedding cake. The tiers are also decorated with baby items, such as bibs, bottles, pacifiers, socks, and toys. Because this is a new option for many people, provide customers with examples of different cakes you have designed on your Web site and what is included with the cake. Allow customers to request different designs or a specific brand of diaper. People who make diaper cakes often also do sideline items, such as diaper wreathes, baby baskets, and baby shower favors. As you business expands, buy diapers in bulk to save money.

Skills needed

Creativity is the most important aspect of this business.

Tips

Consider ways you can expand this type of "cake" into other areas, such as wedding showers and birthdays.

Where to find more information

Diaper Cakes by Becca (**www.diapercakesbybecca.com**) is a prime example of how you can turn your creativity into a profitable business.

#168 *Bridal Shower and Wedding Favors*

Business overview

Anyone who is involved with the wedding industry or was recently married knows a great deal of money is spent on weddings. The average wedding is $20,000 and has approximately 175 guests. With more than two and a half million weddings per year in the United States alone, the wedding industry is bound to be lucrative. Depending on your creativity and entrepreneurial spirit, you can offer the bride and her bridesmaids a wide range of products that fit the wedding's theme and budget. Put your "personalization" hat on and make a list of everything you can offer, such as bridal shower favors, bridal shower games, centerpieces corresponding to the color and theme of the wedding, individualized wedding favors, place cards, flower petals/rice packets, and bridesmaid's gifts. Most brides spend about $400 on favors alone. You can buy wholesale favors from a multitude of companies.

Skills needed

Creativity and a distinctive marketing plan is the most important aspect when starting this business.

Tips

You should offer at least 25 different items that can be customized, as well as a catalog of additional products.

Where to find more information

The search engine **www.partypop.com** is strictly for American wedding favors suppliers.

Sideline Businesses

#169 Personalized Candy Wrapper

With computer design software, it is now easy to offer personalized services from your own home, rather than through a printing company. Many Web sites offer personalized candy wrapping. The candy can be chocolate bars, lollypops, or any other candies the customer requests. There are many different target markets for this business, such as weddings, baby or bridal showers, reunions, retirement parties, graduations, and business functions.

#170 *Custom Bridal Veils/Hair Flowers*

Business overview

As can be seen in the latest TV reality shows, marriage ceremonies have become more luxurious than ever. Brides are concerned about all aspects of their event. To make their wedding gown unique, brides are wearing one-of-a-kind veils and headpieces to precisely match their wedding gown. You can also make silk hair accessories and flowers for the bridesmaids' dresses. To make professionally decorated wedding veils, you need a talent for design and excellent sewing skills, as well as knowledge of what fashion, length, and fabric will be most flattering on the bride and will match the gown. Whether the bride decides on a traditional veil, a pearl tiara, or something completely different, you should be able to provide it. The bride may even decide to mix a vintage and modern look, such as with a veil and glamorous flower peacock. Your couture wedding veils need to feature meticulous detail with only the finest quality fabrics and decorations. They can be beaded by hand with crystals, or decorated with silk bias ribbon, exquisite embroidery, or lace.

You will be consulting with the bride to create a unique creation that will become a family heirloom. In addition to a standard sewing machine, you may need a serging machine for seam finishing and materials, such as pearls, beads, lace, and ribbons that can be handcrafted perfectly into the comb or headpiece. Making these designer veils not only gives you the opportunity to be creative, but also plays a special role in the bride's memorable day. Include a photo of each bride and her unique veil on your Web site. Your biggest challenge is to create a high-quality custom veil at a highly affordable cost. Devote extra time to thoroughly research your wholesale options.

Skills needed

Being a skilled seamstress is important in this business. Creativity and patience are important when working with brides.

Tips

You may want to design first communion veils as a sideline. Sometimes, the bride uses her veil as a centerpiece or favor theme. If so, you may want to discuss this with her an additional service.

Where to find more information

Veil Artistry (**www.veilartistry.com**) is a unique example of this business. Visit their Web site for an idea of how you can get started in this industry.

#171 *Reunion Organizer*

Business overview

As a reunion organizer, you will be responsible for planning the event, as well as finding people associated with high schools or colleges, families, organizations, or businesses. To find "lost" individuals, you will use Internet phone directories, search engines, social networking sites, and databases, as well as information from the sponsors of the event. You will also help find facilities where the event can be held, send out invitations, assemble a guest list, and coordinate the event. You may even attend the reunion to help make sure your plans run smoothly.

Skills needed

In this business, you need to be a great researcher and must enjoy the long hours that must be dedicated to scouring resources online.

Tips

As with any events, things can always go wrong the last minute. Consider contingencies in case of weather problems, and make a list of back-up facilities, just in case.

Where to find more information

Entrepreneur online has a helpful article on getting started with this business at **www.entrepreneur.com/businessideas/29.html**.

#172 *Reminder Service*

Business overview

With our hectic schedules, it is often difficult to remember birthdays, anniversaries, and other special events and holidays. A reminder service can either send clients an e-mail about upcoming important dates, or actually send out the greeting cards for their clients. This is a business with very little overhead costs. Your customers for this reminder service can be consumers and/or businesses. There are many businesses, for example, that send birthday cards to their clients or customers. You will assist your clients with managing the entire process of sending greeting cards to their vendors, customers/clients, and employees for a number of different occasions. If they are consumers, you will send cards to their family members and friends.

You will need a software system to notify you when e-mails or cards need to go out, or when customers need to be contacted. This will need to be linked to your name and address lists. If you are sending cards out through the mail, buy the cards in bulk, or design them yourself with a computer greeting card package. Offering a personalized or fully customized greeting card service would be a big plus. You can add personal photographs or information about the person receiving the card, and you can charge clients a fee for a year's service.

Like with many other online-based services, you can earn additional income by allowing advertisers to feature their related products and services on ads for your Web site.

Skills needed

Organization and reliability is a must. People are turning to you because they do not have the time to keep everything organized. Creativity and computer design skills are needed if you decide to offer customized cards.

Tips

This is a repeat business, so remind your customers at the end of each year to renew their subscription. Do not forget to send cards to your customers, as well. They should be remembered on their own birthdays and anniversaries.

Check all mail and e-mail addresses and the spelling of names with the client, and double-check them through telephone directories.

Where to find more information

HassleMe (**www.hassleme.co.uk**) is a unique example of a reminder service.

Chapter 26

Writers

#173 | Blog Writer

Business overview

Blogs have recently become as important as Web sites. Blogs give merchants a way to establish expertise and credibility with their customers and to encourage visitors to return to the Web site for additional information, products, and services. Many people have writing talent, but blog writing is unique. You need to know the subject thoroughly, because you are writing to people who have a strong interest in this topic. You also need to research stories, news, and information, and condense all of this information into a short and readable blog. If you want to be a blog writer, it is important to be able to write in an interesting and conversational style that builds readership for your client's business. You also need to know the topic well enough to be able to provide your own "take" and personal viewpoint on the issue. By offering your own perspective, you will encourage visitors to comment on a regular basis and build a dialogue between the Web site and the readers. This will help your client build a larger potential customer base and generate traffic to their Web site.

Skills needed

In addition to being able to write about a specific topic, you need to encourage readers to want more information and to send in their own comments. Blog writers should be able to get copy out very quickly and in large quantities.

Tips

Blog writers should research which blog topics are most in need of writers and specialize in one of those areas. If you are ever asked to write a blog on a topic not in your area of expertise, do not say no. Find a writer who specializes in that field and who is willing to be a subcontractor. Also look into featuring paid advertisers on your page after you draw in a regularly substantial audience.

Where to find more information

The International Webmasters Association (**www.iwanet.org**) is a nonprofit that provides educational and certification standards for Web professionals.

#174 Freelance Writer

Business overview

If you enjoy writing and either have a specialty area or are a generalist, there is always a need for freelance writers — both on the Web and in traditional media, such as newspapers and book publishing. Even though the world is increasingly using electronic communication vehicles, print is still very important. Writers are a dime a dozen, but good writers are much rarer. On the Web, writers are needed for Web sites, blogs, e-zines, e-mails, newspapers, magazines, and advertising. Offline, writers are working on brochures, books, magazines, newsletters, and newspapers. Before starting your official business, create a portfolio of your work. Your clients will want to see samples of your writing. Consider whether you have the ability to write on a general list of subjects, or whether you have a specialty. Determine what services you can offer to differentiate you from other writers.

Skills needed

To be a successful freelance writer, you must write strong, persuasive, informative, and entertaining copy. Meeting deadlines is critical. You must understand your target audience and write directly to their informational needs. You must have excellent grammar, and be able to adhere to whatever style (AP, MLA) is required.

Tips

Do not get discouraged with unreturned e-mails, calls, or negative responses. This goes along with the business. Keep making contacts, and the work will come.

Where to find more information

The Editorial Freelancers Association (**www.the-efa.org**) is a nonprofit resource for editorial specialists and those who hire them. JournalismJobs. com (**www.journalismjobs.com**) and Elance (**www.elance.com**) are also good resources for finding journalism work online.

Sideline Businesses

#175 – 182 Writer

- **Freelance editor:** Involves making editorial and grammatical changes to copy already written.

Sideline Businesses

- **Freelance cartooner:** Involves combining artistic and written creativity in the form of a cartoon.

- **Freelance photographer**: Involves taking pictures for a wide variety of individual, business, and corporate clients.

- **Freelance illustrator**: Involves creating hand-drawn and computer-aided drawings for print and electronic purposes.

- **Freelance joke writer:** Involves writing humorous material for radio, television, and special occasions.

- **Freelance speechwriter:** Involves producing speeches for business and professional presenters.

- **Freelance graphic artist**: Involves designing print and electronic designs and layouts.

- **Freelance computer programmer:** Involves developing programs and scripts for specific business and personal needs.

CASE STUDY: SHARYN SCULLY

Sharyn Scully, Owner
A Touch of Color Make-Up
Shelton, CT
203-929-6024
www.atouchofcolormakeup.com

#183 **A Touch of Color Make-Up**

Many freelancers use their Web site to promote and expand their business, but also have an offline "brick-and-mortar" office. Sharyn Scully, a freelance makeup artist, operates her Web site **www.atouchofcolor-makeup.com**, which provides information on her education and training, experience, services, and upcoming special events. She has been a makeup artist and cosmetology educator for nearly 20 years, holding 14 different certifications and having freelanced and consulted for many companies, including Christian Dior, Estée Lauder, Sebastian International, Aveda, and Gosh Cosmetics. Now, she spends most of her time applying skin care and makeup for both men and women for special events, such as weddings, theatrical roles, holiday parties, glamour makeovers, corporate functions, and teenage and young adult functions.

In the past, Scully also created, built, and sold a successful dog-sitting and pet-care business, so she understands the importance of having a strong Web presence. "Even if a business is not actually selling a product or service online, it is important to have a Web site. With so many people searching online instead of in traditional ways, such as the *Yellow Pages,* being on the Internet is essential," she said.

#184 Writing Family Histories

Business overview

Many families want to interview their older family members before their stories and memories are lost. As with genealogical research, some people need a consultant to help them learn the basics of interviewing family members, compiling stories, and writing family histories. Other people may need writing and editorial services. If you are a writer with experience in biographies and autobiographies, and an interest and ability in telephone interviews, you may want to consider this business. With this career, you will be asked to ghostwrite a family history, personal memoir, biography, autobiography, or stories of a person or family. You might only conduct interviews, and give a CD or transcript of the interviews to the client.

But you may also be asked to research the history of an organization, or a business celebrating a special anniversary or compiling a marketing report. You may actually do more than writing. It may be necessary to help people remember memories from their life experiences and draw them out through a memory retrieval process. This frequently includes in-depth interviewing to stimulate remembrances, recall long-forgotten incidences, and confirm other people's memories. Your final written piece may be a book of separate stories or interviews, an actual biography or autobiography, informational reports, newspaper or magazine article, or manuscript to be printed.

Skills needed

Advanced writing and researching skills are necessary in this business.

Tips

This business lends itself to selling materials to help individuals who want to do this on their own. You can sell e-books or CDs containing interviewing tips, for example. Be sure to have excerpts of some of your written materials, as well as testimonials from pleased clients available for potential clients. It is difficult to determine costs for some of these services, especially when you are writing for consumers rather than businesses. Get a full description of the project from a potential client before quoting any prices.

Where to find more information

The National Association of Professional Genealogists (**www.apgen.org**) promotes learning, ethical standards, and services of its members.

Sideline Businesses

#185 Selling E-books

E-books, on every subject imaginable, are available through Web sites and book dealers, such as Amazon and Barnes & Noble. You can create an e-book inexpensively and sell it for a large profit. There are so many e-books already written — some of them are even free to reproduce and sell to others — that it is not necessary to write your own. However, if you have expertise in a particular niche, write your own e-

Sideline Businesses

book and sell it on your Web site. If you are not a writer by nature, but have a topic you believe to be marketable, you can easily hire a freelance writer to compose it for you. Your e-book should have a cover, and the text of the book should be easily designed to include visuals, if necessary. You can distribute your e-book through online bookstores, sell it through social networking and forums, or even upload it to Amazon's new electronic reader, Kindle.

Chapter 27

Relocation and Real Estate Services

#186 | Vacant House/Apartment Cleaning

Business overview

Often, tenants vacate apartments and rental homes without cleaning the space, and apartment management or homeowners usually hire someone to clean before prospective new tenants arrive. This is a very inexpensive business to start because it is mostly labor-intensive. To build a cleaning service targeting a particular geographical area, you need to market your business traditionally offline as well as through the Internet. Your online marketing goal is to have your business listed high among search engines. You Web site should include a brief overview of your services, testimonials, and contact information. Depending on your state, you may need a license to provide cleaning services. You will also need liability insurance, especially if you work with major apartment complexes. The homes you clean will be in varied states of clean. Some may have swept the floor or cleaned the carpet, but did not disinfect the bathrooms, and others may not only be extremely dirty, but still have remaining items, such as furniture, that will need to be removed. You should be hesitant to set prices for a project before seeing the home. Once you get a request, look at the property and then call back the client with a quote based on the amount of time expected to complete the cleaning.

Skills needed

You should have advanced knowledge of cleaning techniques and products. Attention to detail is especially important here.

Tips

Find ways to cut your cleaning time. If you spend too much time, you will not be paid enough for your services. Another option for this business is make additional income by charging advertisers to appear on your site. Many Web sites offering services such as this make an income in this manner. Advertisers will pay to advertise on a site that draws in a frequent and large number of customers. Market to advertisers that relate to the area of business you are covering.

Where to find more information

The National Community of Professional Cleaners (**http://cleaningassociation.com**) is an organization for cleaning businesses.

#187 | Senior Relocation Services

Business overview

The senior population is rapidly growing, as the baby boomers move into their 60s. Many of these individuals will be looking for other living arrangements, from a smaller home to assisted living facilities. They either do not have family to help, or their children and other members are too busy running their own lives. In this business, you can help your clients find another place to live by networking with realtors, apartment managers, and senior living facilities, or you can jump in after the new location has been decided to help coordinate the particulars of the move. The next steps include determining what items will be sold through auction, resale stores, print/online classifieds, or estate sales, and which items will be given to charity or remain with the owner. You will make arrangements for whatever decisions are made, and either pack or throw out the remaining items. You will also help your client find a mover and pack the materials yourself, or oversee the company moving the client's possessions. In addition, you are responsible for any other moving arrangements, such as the stopping or starting of utilities, change-of-address cards, storage, and pets. You may also need to find someone to clean the residence, and you might also help decorate the new living accommodations.

Skills needed

Excellent customer service and research skills are imperative in this business.

Tips

Hire an attorney to write the contracts and discuss issues of liability. Find out from your city what business licenses or permits are required. Also explore the ever-present option of featuring paid advertisements on your Web site if you start drawing in a regular audience.

Where to find more information

MoveSeniors.com (**www.moveseniors.com**) is a good example of this business.

Sideline Businesses

#188   General Relocation Services

A relocation service assists clients with planning all aspects of an upcoming move. It can be difficult to arrange for a move while continuing to work and take care of the family matters. Clients can easily find a relocation service online who can handle most of the work, quickly and efficiently. You can customize your service to a number of different fields, depending on how much time you have, including medical specialists, corporate accounts, families, military, graduate students, or you can decide to help any or all of these individuals, depending on resources and strategy.

#189   Roommate Finder

In cities where there are several universities, students are constantly looking for roommates, or to sublet their apartments when they leave for the summer. Other students are looking for places to live. A roommate matching service will connect these two groups of people. This is entirely a Web-based business. People come to your site, sign up as a member, and fill out a profile about themselves and the apartment they have available, or the apartment they need. Members will be charged a fee for the days they use your service, or they can be charged a fee per match. When a person finds a match, the membership can be canceled. Another option for this business is to offer customers a free Web site for finding roommates, and make money by charging advertisers to appear on your site. Many Web sites offering services such as this make an income in this manner. Advertisers pay to advertise on a site that attracts a large number of customers, so try marketing to advertisers that relate to the area of business you are covering, such as apartment complexes and moving companies.

#190   Apartment/House Locator for Renters

Business overview

In this business, you will be working closely with potential renters. Your business will help renters search for rental apartments, condominiums, or houses in the desired price range and area indicated by your client. People register with your Web site and complete a form specifying their particular needs. Your goal is to find several available sites to fit their specifications and set up appointment times for them to see the locations. You can charge your client an hourly fee for your time, or you can provide this service for a one-time fee to the client, then contract with the apartment or homeowner for an additional fee if the contract is signed. Also see if advertisers are interested in appearing on your site for additional income.

Skills needed

Excellent research skills are necessary when working in this business. An advanced knowledge of the Internet is necessary to create and operate a Web site for this business.

Tips

Increase your income by building referral networks with companies that complement relocation services, such as moving and furniture businesses. Use this service in areas where there is a constant flow of relocation, such as an area with a large university nearby. Make sure you have an attorney draft a contract for agreements with the renters and/or the person renting the property.

Where to find more information

Apartments.com (**www.apartments.com**) is an excellent example of how to get started in this business.

Chapter 28

Each Niche Stands Alone

CASE STUDY: KEN AHRONI

Ken Ahroni, President
Lucky Break Wishbone Corp.
Seattle, WA
866-582-5994

CLASSIFIED CASE STUDIES
directly from the experts

#191 Lucky Break Wishbone Corp.

Ken Ahroni's 47th birthday just happened to fall on Thanksgiving in 1999. During his family's traditional holiday dinner, he began to reminisce about his life thus far. He had been quite fortunate with his 20-year career in product development, but he wanted a change. Eyeing the wishbone on that now-bare turkey, he had one of those "Aha!" moments and thought, "Why is there only one wishbone, when there are so many people who want to make wishes? How many siblings fight over the wishbone every year? Having to wait for it to dry on the windowsill is a drag. There has to be a better way."

Ahroni did not ignore his bright idea, as many people are apt to do. He determined that even if 1 percent of the millions of people who went online were interested, he would have a hit. He invested his resources into a true niche: plastic wishbones that break just like the real thing. His company's tagline reads, "It's time you got a Lucky Break!" It took several years to wrap up his consulting business — which by then he had run successfully for 25 years — and to follow up on his wishbone idea by producing and packaging the wishbones in an American manufacturing facility.

The wishbones have been a big success with the media and, more importantly, with consumers in stores nationwide and online. They are enjoyed year-round for a variety of celebrations, like weddings and home and office parties, and as stocking stuffers — and not just at Thanksgiving. Lucky Break® Wishbones are appreciated by carnivores, but especially vegetarians, because there is "no fowl, so no foul." Thus, in both 2005 and 2006, Ahroni's business jumped tenfold (1,000 percent each year), and continues to grow, even with the current economic slowdown. He attributes this, in part, to his "Proudly Made in the USA" product.

Of course, Ahroni believes strongly in the power of niche products. Coming up with a good idea, however, is only part of the successful equation. "It's a tough world, and you have to be strong not to be chewed up," Ahroni said. In this sort of business, one must continually keep current with the market and have high-quality customer service. Excellent organizational skills, follow-through, and a competitive drive are essential. Marketing in every way possible is a must as well — you have to let people know you have a good product. Ahroni encourages others to follow their gut and take a chance on their own creative niche ideas. He hopes everyone gets a "lucky break," too.

Sideline Businesses

#192 – 199 The Latest Niches

Throughout this book, you have heard the word "niche" over and over again. This is because of its importance to the success of a present-day Web site. The significant thing to remember about a niche it that it is different from all Web businesses. Here are some examples of sites that could effectively target a niche market:

- **Did you hear about the party?:** Come to a Web site where users can list any party or upcoming event they want others to attend — for free. Such activities may include college reunions, club meetings, concerts, birthday celebrations, house parties, and dances. It is a reliable way to let others in on the fun.

- **Saying "I do" beside the ocean waves:** Here are tips on planning the perfect outdoor wedding while keeping the costs relatively low. This site features outside weddings versus traditional, formal ones.

- **The ins and outs of "pain-in-the-neck" tenants:** Is a potential apartment tenant going to pay his or her rent? Or does he or she have a history of paying late or not at all? On this site, property owners work together and compare information on problem or fraudulent tenants.

- **First Judge Judy, now online court:** At this new jury site, users can settle simple grievances, such as who was right in an argument. Both parties face the jury, the Internet public, and plead their cases. The winner gets an agreed-upon pay off, such as free dinner or tickets to the local football game.

- **If you loved this Web site, you will also love…:** The one objective of this new site is to help users find other sites that are similar to the ones they already like. They can follow people with similar interests through the maze of millions of unknown Internet sites.

Sideline Businesses

- **Will work just for the experience:** It is becoming increasingly difficult to find an internship, let alone a real job. This site lists both available internships and the individuals who want them.

- **A step-by-step guide on step-by-steps:** Want a manual on how to do something, such as ow to put your kid's bike together or how to make a French crème brûlée? Find every instruction manual on this site.

- **Niche of the niche of the niche**: What is the latest niche Web site? Go to this Web site to found out the latest niche sites.

Conclusion

As you begin your journey for starting your own online business, remember that those listed in this book are only examples. Some are very broad and can be "niched" down, and others are such a specific niche that it would be difficult to be duplicate them. If you have the specific skill set needed for one of these businesses, and it is of interest to you, then go for it.

I have talked with at least 60 Web site owners for my books about online Web businesses. Some of the business owners work part-time and like the additional money; some are just starting and only making minimal income; several are maintaining decent revenues and enjoy the fact that they are working on their own; and a number of the people are true online entrepreneurs. These latter individuals put in long hours and great effort. They started with very few funds and were able to build an incredibly lucrative business.

The Internet is a strange phenomenon; I have learned it is not so much the product that sells, but the person behind that product. Yes, buyers look at prices, but if the prices are comparable, they look at the Web site, the information, and the person who stands behind that product or service. By offering your customers or clients vital information through a Web site, blog, or on Twitter, you increase your online presence and credibility. When people are looking for a product they can get from several different merchants, they will go with the Web site with whom they have established a relationship.

One other word about the Internet: In addition to Web sites for a service or product, there are many nonprofit organizations, business associations, government-related sites, and personal causes. They sell memberships and offer such services as books, conferences, and statistical reports for a specific group of people. For example, I have started my own online program, Complete Freedom from Anxiety and Panic™, to help the millions of Americans who are struggling with depression and anxiety. My "product" includes a book, downloadable reports, and telephone interviews, Webinars, and teleconferences with psychologists about confronting different forms of anxiety. This is a wider niche that is of personal concern, and you can follow this route as well if you have something that you personally want to support.

Will you be able to make millions of dollars in sales? This is a question you may want to keep in the back of your mind, yet it should not be the motivation for starting your online business; rather, "success" should be your objective — however you define it. When writing your mission and vision statements, you are defining how you measure success. Keep on that path and put in the effort, and you can achieve your success.

Appendix

Sample Business Plan

Publisher's Note to Readers: Please note that this is a sample business plan and is meant for your educational use. This business plan is a simple example of how a business plan should be formatted and the type of information that you should include. This sample is shortened; many professional business plans are much longer in length.

Business plan for Pet Sitting by Milly

June 2008, Confidential

Development Team: Milly Peterson

1234 Wealth Lane, Camden, ND 90002

Phone: 555-555-9999, Fax: 555-555-1234

www.petsittingbymilly.com, info@petsittingbymilly.com

Executive summary

This business proposal describes the plans for operating a pet sitting business named Pet Sitting by Milly, with an office and pet boarding facility located at the personal residence of owner Milly Peterson, at 1234 Wealth Lane Camden, ND 90002. The objective of this proposal is to request a $50,000 working line of credit to be used for ongoing operating costs and to outline the businesses long-term marketing strategies.

Pet Sitting by Milly is a full-service pet sitting business offering full-time in-home care, part-time in-home care, and care at the on-site pet boarding facility in the Camden area. Levels of service completely depend on the needs of the pet and the wants of the owner.

Pet Sitting by Milly is committed to offering personable, warm service to customers and their pets. Services at Pet Sitting by Milly are unique and considerably different than what is provided at most boarding kennels. With the majority of boarding services, pets are kept in small kennels, allowed outside to run and play for a very limited amount of time daily, and limited in the amount of human interaction they receive during their stays. Typically, pets are left at boarding kennels during weekends and holidays. These, unfortunately, are the times when many boarding services such as kennels or veterinarian's offices are closed. Staff comes to the office at scheduled times during these weekends or holidays to feed and walk the animals, but usually leave little time to interact with the animals personally. More and more pet owners are deciding that their pets should receive the same attention away from home as they do when at home, and that general pet boarding services will no longer suit their needs.

Fortunately, residents of the Camden area have a budget-friendly alternative. Pet sitting in itself is an entirely different way of caring for pets than traditional boarding. At Pet Sitting by Milly, pets receive one-on-one attention. Whether services are performed at the customer's home or at the on-site facility, customers can relax knowing that their pets are being cared for in a home environment while they are away.

Objectives

Pet Sitting by Milly is committed to straying from traditional pet-boarding practices and taking care of beloved pets in a way that mimics the pet's home environment. Each pet is different and needs different amounts of attention and care. Pet Sitting by Milly is committed to knowing the pet personally in order to fulfill the specific needs of each pet.

Mission

It is the mission of Pet Sitting by Milly to provide customers with the peace of mind that comes along with knowing their pet is in an experienced, safe environment while providing services that mimic the comfort and stability that comes with a home environment.

Keys to success

The keys to Pet Sitting by Milly's success are as follows: Provide services that mimic a pet's home environment in order to instill comfort and stability. Provide customers the peace of mind that comes along with knowing their pet is in a home environment. Surround pets with experienced, knowledgeable staff and veterinarians while still providing one-on-one, personable service.

Statement of purpose

This business proposal describes the plans for operating a pet sitting business named Pet Sitting by Milly, with an office and pet boarding facility located at the personal residence of owner Milly Peterson, at 1234 Wealth Lane Camden, ND 90002. The objective of this proposal is to request a $50,000 working line of credit to be used for ongoing operating costs and to outline the businesses long-term marketing strategies.

Company summary

Pet Sitting by Milly opened in 2004 by Milly Peterson as a sole proprietorship. As the sole owner of the company, Peterson is a licensed veterinarian, and her personal home is a licensed boarding facility within the city of Camden and the state of North Dakota.

Pet Sitting by Milly offers full-time in-home care, part-time in-home care, and care in the on-site facility. Pet Sitting by Milly is proud to offer customers a non-traditional boarding service, while still providing medical attention to all animals if necessary. Pet Sitting by Milly offers services to a wide variety of animals, from cats and dogs, snakes and iguanas, to goats and llamas, tarantulas and rabbits. Different animals require different amounts of care and attention. With many different levels of service, Pet Sitting by Milly can serve the needs of most animals, big or small. With a veterinarian always available, even full-time in-home care allows for the attention of a medical professional if necessary. And because Pet Sitting by Milly loves repeat customers and always wants pets to feel at ease in their surroundings, customers are assigned a specific care-giver who will always be the person to look after their pet.

Company ownership

The company is owned and directly operated by Milly Peterson. Opening the company in 2004, Milly Peterson formed the company as a sole proprietorship.

Owner Milly Peterson graduated with a degree from North Dakota State College in animal sciences and business. She went on to get her veterinarian's degree from NDSC. After working in a veterinarian's clinic in Camden for 10 years, Peterson opened Pet Sitting by Milly. Peterson has received many awards for her outstanding veterinary services. Believing that she could offer more to the world of pet boarding and animal care, Peterson decided to open Pet Sitting by Milly to provide customers with a non-traditional approach to pet boarding.

Pet Sitting by Milly employs five veterinarians who are on-call day and night for service calls. These veterinarians can be dispatched to a customer's home if necessary. Also employed is a staff of licensed pet-sitters who attend to the animals in the customer's home or in the pet sitting facility.

This staff is available in day and night shifts at the on-site facility or for an extended period of time at a customer's home. An office staff is also employed at the pet sitting facility.

Company location and facility

Pet Sitting by Milly operates out of the personal residence of owner Milly Peterson at 1234 Wealth Lane Camden, ND 90002. The facility is centered around the personal residence of owner Milly Peterson, with a full veterinarian's office on site as well as facilities for the animals, such as a fenced pool and dog-run, a cat playhouse, and a kennel facility for pets that prefer sleeping in the comfort of a closed area.

Legal form of business

The legal name of the business is Pet Sitting by Milly and operates as a sole proprietorship, as registered in the state of North Dakota.

Services

Pet Sitting by Milly offers several different levels of service to customers — full-time in-home care, part-time in-home care, and care in the on-site facility. Pet Sitting by Milly also offers veterinarian services to customers not participating in boarding services. Customers can have numerous services performed while their pets are in the care of the professionals at the facility, including nail clippings, teeth cleanings, annual shots, grooming, regular flea and heartworm treatments, and much more. Pet Sitting by Milly specializes in the care of dogs and cats, but veterinarians at the facility are trained in the care of many other types of animals. Because different animals require different types of care and attention, Pet Sitting by Milly provides personable services that are unique to the animal type. Below is a description of the services offered with each type of care.

Full-time in-home care is probably the most unique of the services offered by Pet Sitting by Milly. This service involves a caregiver providing care to a customer's pet in the customer's home for an extended period of time. With the full-time in-home care, customers are typically away from home for an extended period of time. The caregiver is much like a live-in nanny for pets. The caregiver lives at the customer's home for the length of time that the customer is away. This service is perfect for pets that need a lot of attention and that cannot be left alone for long periods of time. Such animals may include elderly dogs or cats, or just animals that are typically more comfortable in their own environment. Pet Sitting by Milly provides these services to customers who would like their pet to stay within the comfort of their own home while they are away. Many animals behave differently when moved to an unfamiliar location with unfamiliar people and animals, and many customers just prefer to have their pet stay within their home. Whatever the customer's reason for taking part in the service, Pet Sitting by Milly is committed to providing care that is not only comfortable, but safe as well. A team of veterinarians is always on-call and can be dispatched to the customer's home should the need arise. Caregivers are always trained and licensed to care for pets. Customers can provide specific instructions for the care of their pets while in the home. Pets are fed, walked, and played with as the customer prefers. Fees for these services are charged on a per-night basis with different fee levels depending upon the specific needs of the animal. Customers are charged an extra fee for more than 3 nights of service. Caregivers and pets are always prescreened to make sure that the two will be compatible living partners. Customers are given a chance to observe their pet's behavior with the caregiver before choosing to participate in the service. Once the customer has decided on a caregiver, the customer will be assigned that specific caregiver for all future sessions.

Part-time in-home care is the perfect choice for customers who want their pets to be able to stay in the comfort of their own home, but who do not need constant supervision on the part of the caregiver. This service is perfect for animals such as cats, dogs that can be trusted to be unattended for long amounts of time or that require less attention, rabbits, and much more. Typically, the caregiver visits the customer's house three to four times a day — once in the morning for a walk and feeding if necessary, once in the afternoon for a walk and playtime, and once in the evening for a walk and feeding. The caregiver typically spends 30 minutes to an hour at the customer's house for each visit, and an extra visit can be arranged if the customer requests. The specific times that the caregiver visits the house is entirely up to the customer and is generally based on the routine of the animal. Many times, customers wish to mimic the routine that the animal is comfortable with, based on the normal times the customer is at home. As with the previous service, a team of veterinarians is always on call, should the need arise, and the pets are cared for exactly as the customer requests. Customers are charged based on the number of visits to the home and the length of time spent at the home. As with the previous service, caregivers are always prescreened to make sure that the animals and caregivers are compatible. The same caregiver will provide service to the customer's house throughout the length of time requested.

A twist on traditional boarding services is provided to customers with the on-site care at Pet Sitting by Milly. This service is great for animals that need constant companionship and get along with a variety of other people and other animals. Unlike traditional boarding facilities where animals are kept in kennels for the majority of the day and staff is only at the facility for feeding and walking, at Pet Sitting by Milly, animals are constantly surrounded by staff. Animals are very rarely kept in kennels during the day and are either at the doggy-pool, in the dog-run, playing games with the staff, or lounging in the open-air, free-roam space provided. As many animals are not use to sleeping in kennels, there are several different options for nighttime care. If the animal is use to sleeping in a kennel, the staff happily accommodates the animal's usual routine, providing plush pillows for the animals to sleep on instead of the hard concrete floor that exists in most boarding facilities. However, if the animal typically has a different sleeping preference, Pet Sitting by Milly is happy to accommodate that request. An open room in the facility has different sleeping arrangements available, such as plush dog beds, pet sofas, cat towers, window hammocks for the cats, or, if the animals prefers, they can lounge on the floor. Animals are always supervised when left alone in an open area, even during the night. Pets are always screened for their behavior among other animals before acceptance at the facility, and if the animal is deemed aggressive, service is either denied or in-home service is recommended. All dogs and cats must be spayed or neutered before they will be accepted into the facility, or else an in-home service is recommended. All animal types are kept separate from the other types to avoid confrontations. Animals are fed to the specifications provided from the customer. Fees are charged on a per-night basis at the facility. A team of veterinarians is always available at the facility, as well as a licensed and trained staff to play with and care for the animal's personal needs.

Pet Sitting by Milly offers non-surgical veterinary services, as well as boarding services. Services can be performed while the animal is in the care of the on-site facility, or animals can be brought to the facility at any time by the customer. Services offered are listed in detail on the company Web site, but in brief here. Pet Sitting by Milly offers grooming, teeth cleaning, nail clipping, flea and heartworm treatments, and much more. Service fees range depending on the type of service and the type of animal.

Market analysis summary

It is estimated that at least 40 million households in the United States own at least one dog, and that Americans will spend $43 billion in 2008 on their pets. More and more Americans are defining their pets as members of their families. With this in mind, most pet owners are willing to spend an exorbitant amount to see that their pet is taken care of. While services offered by Pet Sitting by Milly are typically more expensive than traditional boarding services, the services offered by the company are unique. As the statistic above show, Pet Sitting by Milly is a good investment and a trend that has rapidly grown popular in the Camden area.

Market segmentation

Services provided by Pet Sitting by Milly are generally regarded as a luxury expense among customers and services are generally marketed toward a middle- to high-income group within the Camden area. With the median income in the Camden area equaling $75,000 annually, services are typically marketed toward the upper-income bracket that has more money for disposable services. With different service levels available, Pet Sitting by Milly is a service that can be used by someone on a tighter budget, however. Also, several promotions that are ongoing will help draw in these new customers. Details of this promotion are covered in the strategy section of this business plan.

Market analysis

As demonstrated below in the pie chart, Pet Sitting by Milly has broken the customer base into four distinct groups based on four different groups of people that use the services of the company. Each section shows where the most and the least amount of profit is made for the business, and also which type of people use the specific services.

As the pie chart below indicates, 49 percent of Pet Sitting by Milly's customer base is made up of customers who use the on-site care provided at the boarding facility. This service is the top seller for the company, bringing in a total of 49 percent of income in 2007. This bracket is largest partly because the facility can accommodate a much larger number of animals than the in-home care services can. With a limited number of caregivers available for in-home service, these services typically automatically produce less income than the other services.

Customers of this bracket are generally two-income families with a median income of $55,000 annually. This market always has the potential to increase as services are marketed to a wider customer base. As this service is generally the least expensive service that the company offers, this service will be marketed to people with a tighter income base. An ongoing promotion for this service will also help to widen the customer base interested in these services.

25 percent of the customer base is made up of customers who use the full-time in-home care services. This service brought in 25 percent of income for the company in 2007. While typically more expensive than the on-site care, this service is highly popular in the Camden area. This service is thought to be the company's specialty and is looked upon as being a status service among the middle- to upper-income groups in the Camden area.

Customers in this bracket are divided nearly 50 percent between two-income and one-income families with a media income level of $64,000 annually. The main means of marketing to this bracket is through word-of-mouth advertising and customer referrals. In order to increase the sales in this bracket, an ongoing referral campaign will be emphasized among current customers.

18 percent of the customer base is made up of customers taking part in part-time in-home care services. This service brought in 18 percent of income for the company in 2007. This service is usually used by customers with less income-producing animals such as reptiles, rabbits, etc., where the animal does not need constant care. These animals typically just need to be fed; therefore, service fees for these animals are less.

Customers in this bracket are generally two-income families with a median income of $52,000 annually. More can be done to increase this bracket and, generally, marketing to a wide variety of potential customers is the more efficient avenue. More public education on this service would be helpful. This would allow customers who would generally leave their pets with a neighbor or friend because of the price of the full-time service to perhaps use this service. More information on the frequency caregivers visit the homes of the animals and the level of comfort the service provides would be helpful to increase sales among this bracket.

8 percent of the customer base is made up of customers who use the non-surgical services of the veterinary facility. The majority of these customers are typically already boarding customers, so their income brackets fall somewhere in the numbers listed above. In order to increase sales in these areas, a marketing campaign will be instituted.

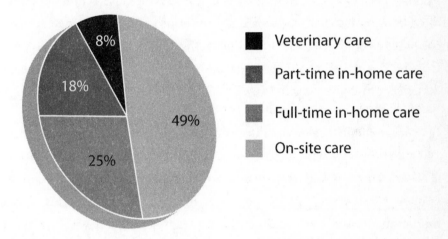

Target market segment strategy and sales strategy

Pet Sitting by Milly is increasingly concerned with connecting with potential clients in order to build a solid customer base that will support the business in the future. While continual advertisement is ongoing to our current customer base, Pet Sitting is currently looking to expand several different customer bases. The marketing strategies for each sales and customer bracket are laid out in the following marketing summary.

In order to increase sales and the customer bracket among the first group, which corresponds with the on-site care, a marketing campaign is underway to bring in new customers to this service. Because service with the company tends to be thought of a service that only high-income earners can afford, Pet Sitting by Milly wants to increase public awareness on the affordability of the on-site care program. Advertisement in the *Camden Daily Journal* is ongoing, as well as a direct mail coupon for 20 percent off a new customer's first visit to Pet Sitting by Milly.

In order to increase sales and the customer bracket among the second group, which corresponds with the full-time in-home care, a referral campaign is underway to bring in new customers. Because the main source of advertising for this service is word-of-mouth and customer referrals, a customer referral program is the optimal way to bring in new customers. Existing customers who refer a new customer to this service will receive a 20 percent discount on a future service.

In order to increase sales and the customer bracket among the third group, which corresponds with the part-time in-home care, a public informational advertisement is underway to educate the potential customer base of the frequency caregivers visit the home for this service and how this service mimics the routine that customers have already set in place with their pets. Many potential customers now leave pets with neighbors or friends when they travel due to personal care and budget limitations. In order to win over this bracket, the advertisement shows that even with part-time care, they can still receive personal care and stay within a budget.

In order to increase sales and the customer bracket among the third group, which corresponds with the on-site veterinary services, a marketing campaign will be instituted to educate potential customers on the services provided. Many potential customers do not know that the company offers non-surgical veterinary services. Advertisement of grooming services will be ongoing. Also, Pet Sitting by Milly has considered hiring a surgical veterinarian for other procedures that the company is unable to do now. Market research into the need and benefits of such an action are ongoing.

Competition

The competition among boarding facilities in the Camden area is limited. There are several veterinary offices in the Camden area, with two offices offering traditional boarding services. Pet Sitting by Milly is the only service that offers in-home services, as well as free-roam care and a 24-hour staff available for pets at all times.

The two veterinary kennels, Smith's Animal Clinic and Keystone Veterinary Services, are by no means direct competition for the company. The service offered among the companies varies heavily, and customers are rarely shared among the three services.

Competitive edge

Pet Sitting by Milly is committed to offering personable, warm service to customer and their pets. Services at Pet Sitting by Milly are unique and considerably different from what is provided at most boarding kennels. With the majority of boarding services, pets are kept in small kennels, allowed outside to run and play for a very limited amount of time daily, and limited in the amount of human interaction they receive during their stays. Typically, pets are left at boarding kennels during weekends and holidays. These, unfortunately, are the times when many boarding services such as kennels or veterinarian's offices are closed. Staff comes to the office at scheduled time during these weekends or holidays to feed and walk the animals, but usually leave very little time to interact with the animals personally. More and more pet owners are deciding that their pets should receive the same attention away from home as they do when at home, and that general pet boarding services will no longer suit their needs.

Fortunately, residents of the Camden area have a budget-friendly alternative. Pet sitting in itself is an entirely different way of caring for pets than the traditional boarding. At Pet Sitting by Milly, pets receive one-on-one attention. Whether services are performed at the customer's home or at the on-site facility, customers can relax knowing that their pets are being cared for in a home environment while they are away.

Bibliography

Bridal Association of America. "Wedding Statistics." **www.bridalassocia-tionofamerica.com/Wedding_Statistics/**

www.Compete.com. **http://siteanalytics.compete.com/amazon. com+walmart.com/?metric=uv**

de Chernatony, L. and McDonald, M. (1992) *Creating Powerful Brands.* Oxford, UK: Butterworth Heinemann.

Fortune "Most Admired Companies of 2006." **www.fortunesmallbusi-ness.com/magazines/fortune/mostadmired/2006/index.html**

Power Reviews **www.powerreviews.com**

Forrester Research *The State of Retailing Online 2008*, the 11th annual Shop.org study. **www.shop.org**

Strategy+Business Magazine "Web 2.0: Profiting from the Threat."

http://74.125.93.132/search?q=cache:7zTiL_WV3aMJ:www.strategy-business.com/article/li00037%3Fgko%3Dacfde+online+consumer+b ehavior,+goes+to+niche+rather+than+large+site&cd=9&hl=en&ct=cl nk&gl=us

Author Biography

During her years as a communication consultant for nonprofit and business clients, Sharon Cohen watched and appreciated the rise of the Internet as it impacted and changed the world, as it did her own life. Once spending most of her time publishing print marketing and information materials and books for nonprofit organizations and corporations, she now communicates online to complete writing projects for businesses; offer grammatical and literary advice to students; interface with newfound associates and old friends worldwide; and find answers to arcane research questions with several Google clicks. With a passion for writing and reading her whole life, she has spent many a day visiting and working in libraries, and perusing and ordering books from Amazon.

She continues to watch with appreciation the way the Internet may be used to enhance world communication and shared learning and bring education and literacy to the global village. Cohen uses her writing skills to help others develop their online businesses through coaching and editorial support with e-books, Web sites, and blogging. Her Web site is **http://online-business-guide.com**. Cohen is also the author of *Amazon*

Income: How Anyone of Any Age, Location, and/or Background Can Build a Highly Profitable Online Business with Amazon and *Yahoo! Income: How Anyone of Any Age, Location, and/or Background Can Build a Highly Profitable Online Business with Yahoo!,* also published by Atlantic Publishing Company in 2009.

Index

C